D0224034

THE GLOBAL ECONOMICS OF SPORT

Sport has become a global business. There is no corner of the Earth that isn't reached by coverage of global sporting mega-events such as the Olympics or the World Cup, events managed by international governing bodies such as the IOC and FIFA that operate like major international businesses. Companies such as Nike now design, produce, distribute and market their products across every continent, while an increasingly important part of every country's sport market is now international in terms of its influences and opportunities.

This book is the first to examine the economics of contemporary sport using the global market as the primary unit of analysis. Starting with a survey of the changing nature of the sport market over the last hundred years, the book explores the difficulties of measuring the true scale and impact of the global sports economy, employing a wealth of empirical data to define and analyse the sports market and all its sub-sectors. In doing so, the book draws on case studies from the UK, Europe, North America and beyond. This book is essential reading for any student or professional with an interest in the economics of sport.

Chris Gratton is Professor of Sports Economics and Director of the Sport Industry Research Centre at Sheffield Hallam University, UK.

Dongfeng Liu is Professor and Associate Dean at the School of Economics and Management, Shanghai University of Sport, China.

Girish Ramchandani is Research Fellow in the Sport Industry Research Centre at Sheffield Hallam University, UK.

Darryl Wilson is a Senior Lecturer in Sport Business Management in the Faculty of Health and Wellbeing, Sheffield Hallam University, UK.

THE GLOBAL ECONOMICS OF SPORT

Chris Gratton, Dongfeng Liu,
Girish Ramchandani and Darryl Wilson

Routledge
Taylor & Francis Group

LONDON AND NEW YORK

First published 2012
by Routledge
2 Park Square, Milton Park, Abingdon, Oxon OX14 4RN

Simultaneously published in the USA and Canada
by Routledge
711 Third Avenue, New York, NY 10017

Routledge is an imprint of the Taylor & Francis Group, an informa business

© 2012 Chris Gratton, Dongfeng Liu, Girish Ramchandani and Darryl Wilson

The right of Chris Gratton, Dongfeng Liu, Girish Ramchandani and Darryl
Wilson to be identified as authors of this work has been asserted by them in
accordance with sections 77 and 78 of the Copyright, Designs and Patents Act
1988.

All rights reserved. No part of this book may be reprinted or reproduced or
utilised in any form or by any electronic, mechanical, or other means, now
known or hereafter invented, including photocopying and recording, or in any
information storage or retrieval system, without permission in writing from the
publishers.

Trademark notice: Product or corporate names may be trademarks or registered
trademarks, and are used only for identification and explanation without intent to
infringe.

British Library Cataloguing in Publication Data
A catalogue record for this book is available from the British Library

Library of Congress Cataloging-in-Publication Data
The global economics of sport / edited by Chris Gratton... [et al.].
p. cm.
1. Sports–Economic aspects –Cross-cultural studies. 2. Sports and globalization–
Cross-cultural studies. I. Gratton, Chris, 1948-
GV716.G545 2012
796.06'91–dc23
2011052008

ISBN: 978-0-415-58618-4 (hbk)
ISBN: 978-0-415-58619-1 (pbk)
ISBN: 978-0-203-80724-8 (ebk)

Typeset in Bembo
by Taylor & Francis Books

CONTENTS

FIGURES

TABLES

1

THE HISTORICAL AND ECONOMIC DEVELOPMENT OF THE SPORT MARKET

Introduction

This book aims to look at how economics can help us to understand and analyse the increasing globalisation of the sport market. This chapter sets the scene for the book by looking at the historical and economic development of the sport market. It will describe how sport prior to the 1960s was predominantly a local activity. Broadcasting rights income, government funding of elite sport, and sponsorship income were negligible. During this period, the sport market was dominated by mass participation sport with the voluntary sector the main supplier. Elite sport was mainly amateur with the exception of some professional team sports where rewards were modest. In the 1960s and 1970s, international sporting competitions became increasingly important, creating the need for national policies and strategies for elite sport. Also the *Sport for all* movement recognised the health and social benefits of sports, creating a need for a national policy for mass participation sport. National agencies for sport were set up in many countries, signalling the increasing importance of government in sport. Since the early 1980s, the sport market has become increasingly global, driven by increasing commercial sector interest in sport and this globalisation of the sport market is the focus of this book. However, let us start by looking back at the history of the development of the sport market prior to these modern developments.

It is generally agreed that England is the birth place of modern sport. Viewed by some as the 'cradle of modern sport', England is the nation that was most influential in developing and moulding games and sport into their current forms (Toohey and Veal 2007). Maguire *et al.* (2002) stated: 'Although there is evidence of cultic or play activities, folk games and recreations in the ancient worlds and civilisations of Europe,

Asia and South America, modern sport, like the steam engine, emerged first in England.' Mandell (1984) goes further:

> We know that almost all the field events of a track meet were invented by English university students. They invented the running broad jump, the triple jump, the hurdles, and steeplechase races. They also established the standard track distances. Englishmen set the distances for swimmers, for rowing competitions, and for horse races of all kinds. By selective breeding Englishmen established the modern race horse and most recognised varieties of sporting dogs. They built the first sporting yachts, racing sculls, and row boats for trained crews. They also devised the first football goal posts, boxing gloves, stopwatches, and most other sporting equipment for which they set the earliest standard dimensions, weights, materials, and so on. Englishmen 'invented' (that is they first wrote down the fixed rules for games which had been variously played earlier) almost all the team games now played from football (both rugby and soccer) to polo. So rapid, and more particularly thorough, have been the advances of these standardised sports and games that it is easy to forget that most of the events, games, and equipment of modern sports are not much more than a hundred years old. Some other field events are of Scottish origins. Until 50 or 60 years ago it was widely assumed that only English-speaking people could enjoy and achieve distinction in sports which are now played and observed everywhere.
>
> (Mandell 1984)

Norbert Elias referred to a 'civilising process' in England in the course of which the rules of sports came more and more to be written down, nationally (subsequently internationally) standardised, more explicit, more precise, more comprehensive, orientated around an ethos of 'fair play' and providing equal chances for all participants to win, and with reducing and/or more strictly controlling opportunities for violent physical contact (Elias and Dunning 1986).

According to Elias and Dunning (1986), modern sports emerged in England in two main phases. The first phase of the seventeenth and eighteenth centuries witnessed the transformation of a variety of pastimes, including cricket, fox hunting, horse racing and boxing, into recognisably modern sports. In the second phase, the early and mid-nineteenth century, soccer, rugby, tennis and track and field began to take on modern forms. During the late nineteenth and early twentieth centuries, many of the international and later global sport organisations (GSOs) began to emerge and also saw the beginning of the modern Olympic Games. This overlapped with a fourth phase that lasted from the 1920s through to the 1960s. It entailed the differential diffusion of English sport forms to continental Europe and to both the formal and informal British Empire (Maguire *et al.* 2002). More recently, beginning in the 1980s, a fifth phase began to unfold. The fourth phase witnessed the continuing growth of international sports competitions but it is the fifth phase that saw the emergence of the global sport market. We look at each of these phases below starting with the emergence of sport in pre-industrial England.

Pre-industrial sport and recreation (pre-1800)

If we go back to the early 1600s, in England we find a picture of the ordinary worker faced with a relatively rich and diverse set of leisure activities. Drinking (alcohol) was virtually a universal activity; holidays were more numerous than they were in early industrial Britain, and some sports – football, cricket, horse racing, boxing, cock-fighting, bull-baiting and dog-fighting – both participant and spectator, were highly popular. Many of these leisure pursuits were complementary: holidays such as Shrove Tuesday, Christmas, or May Day were the occasions for long drinking sessions where sports were organised for entertainment. The ale-house, or tavern, was the centre for many of these activities: one survey of South Lancashire villages in 1647 indicated that there was an average of one ale-house for every 12 households (or approximately one per 57 inhabitants) (Malcolmson 1973).

However, people in the seventeenth century would not have identified leisure as we do today. Leisure in modern industrial Britain is something that derives its definition from work: a leisure activity is something we do in non-work time. In seventeenth-century, rural, agricultural Britain, there was no clear distinction between work and leisure. Agricultural production itself followed the rhythm of the seasons with times of hard, intense work (e.g. during harvest) followed by quiet periods. During these less active times, leisure and work would be occasionally indistinguishable. It was certainly common for agricultural workers to drink while they were working. Documents from the time record complaints that workers were observing 'Saint Monday', that is taking Monday off for extra leisure time (often because they had worked the whole of Saturday). It seemed that workers often 'voted with their feet' for a five-day week (Reid 1967). Many sporting activities would take place in these periods of 'stolen' leisure time. Equally, many people were engaged in sports during the working day out in the fields.

Despite the fact that both spectator and participant sport were regular activities, they were unrecognisable from the same activities today. Football as practised then had no designated pitch or goals and the teams could consist of hundreds of people. No sport market existed. Nobody paid any money to participate in sport or to spectate. There was expenditure on gambling related to sport and on alcohol consumed either watching or playing it.

Early industrial Britain (1800–1850)

The movement from agriculture to manufacturing industry, involving the movement of the population from a rural to an urban environment, completely altered leisure in Britain. The most significant change was in the availability of leisure time. Factory work typically involved a six-day week, with working days of at least 12 hours for men, women and children alike. There was no seasonal rhythm to this work – every week was the same. Holidays also decreased: in 1750 the Bank of England closed on 47 holidays; by 1830 this had decreased to 18, and by 1834 it closed on only four – Good Friday, Christmas Day, and the first days of May and November. During the same period, many of the popular recreations of pre-industrial Britain had virtually disappeared.

The rise of factory working not only reduced the availability of leisure time for the average worker; income was also a major constraint. In the towns and cities, leisure activities increasingly had to be paid for, and the early industrial workers hardly received a subsistence income. The recreations of the working class in this period were largely restricted to the pleasures of the tavern, alcohol and prostitution. These activities were predominantly male-orientated; leisure activities for women were even more restricted.

Time and money were not the only constraints facing the new industrialised working classes. Space was also a major constraint. Many sports, football in particular, could not flourish in the new industrial towns because of the lack of space. These activities still survived in rural areas, but by 1851 the majority of the English population lived in towns and cities.

Coalter, Long, and Duffield (1986) argue that industrialisation created a new force towards greater control of leisure activities: 'New forms of work organisation required a new sense of time and work discipline which were in opposition to many popular pastimes (Thompson 1967). The systematic organisation of work into specified times and places required reciprocal forms of "rational" non-work activities.'

As indicated earlier, work and leisure time were never completely separated in an agricultural economy. Manufacturing industry, however, required a complete separation of work and leisure. Coalter *et al.* (1986) indicate that whereas drinking while working in the fields was commonplace, drinking while working with the machinery in the new factories was both disruptive and dangerous. Industrialisation involved heavy capitalisation and working with this capital not only required a sober workforce but also it required that workforce to work long hours so that the capital equipment was kept fully employed.

The role of government in the early nineteenth century was to support the new manufacturing industries in providing an effective labour workforce. This involved 'criminalising and suppressing popular recreations' and 'regulating and rationally organising the temporal parameters of leisure' (Coalter *et al.* 1986). As far as suppressing popular recreations was concerned, some blood sports (e.g. cock-fighting, bull-baiting and dog-fighting) were made illegal. Leisure time was regulated and 'rationally organised' by the passing of various factory acts which established clear divisions between work time and leisure time. In this early period of industrialisation therefore, the role of government was one of suppressing popular working-class sports and recreations.

If this was the picture of leisure for the new urbanised working class, the rich had a wider choice of leisure pursuits. They were the leisured classes with time and money to do as they wished. Although concern for animals led to legislation to ban cock-fighting and bull-baiting, other activities such as fox hunting, shooting and fishing were considered respectable for gentlemen.

It was not only the very rich, however, who enjoyed a wider choice of leisure activities. The Industrial Revolution had created a new affluent class, the industrialists, who, though having less leisure time than the aristocracy, did have the money to adopt the leisure pursuits of the very rich. It is noticeable that their choice was to copy the leisure habits of the aristocracy – a process of 'filtering-down' of leisure activities that is identifiable throughout the history of leisure.

The new rich also followed the aristocracy in another way: they sent their male sons to the elite public schools. It was these schools that played a crucial role in the development of sport in England. Holt (1989) describes how the top public schools initially 'saw the potential of sport as a source of discipline and morality', but eventually 'sport ceased to be a means to a disciplinary end and became an end in itself. The culture of athleticism steadily came to dominate the whole system of elite education.' The top public schools had sports every day. Individual schools codified the rules and these eventually became standardised across the schools as they started to play each other in these sports. Pupils from these schools went to on to Oxford and Cambridge and these institutions also became much more serious about sport. The first Oxford and Cambridge cricket match took place in 1827 and the first boat race between the two universities in 1829 (Holt 1989).

For these more affluent classes, there was a significant lack of government suppression of their sport and recreation activities. The more affluent were also starting to spend significant sums on their sporting activities contributing to the beginning of the sport market.

The re-emergence of mass leisure (1850–1914)

As the nineteenth century progressed, the twin constraints of time and money were gradually eased for the mass of the English population and leisure activities began to expand. By the 1850s, fewer people worked on Saturday afternoons and, because of the strong influence of the sabbatarian lobby keeping Sunday a rest day, it became the regular sport and recreation afternoon. Initially, it was the better paid skilled working class who led the move to a more varied leisured lifestyle. A new influence, technology, emerged to shape the leisure demands of the masses with increased time and money. The same technology that led to the Industrial Revolution and the restrictions of factory working, then started to widen the opportunities for enjoyment. The largest single change was the coming of the railways. The day out to the seaside became a mass leisure pursuit, made possible by this new, relatively fast cheap form of transport.

But it was not only technology that was changing. Real wages increased by about 40 per cent between 1860 and 1875 and by a further 33 per cent between 1875 and 1900. The idea that time should be set aside for leisure interests was encapsulated in the Bank Holiday Act of 1870 which established a day's holiday in August. Although originally only intended for bank workers, it was quickly adopted as a general holiday. It was this day in particular that became the day of the mass trip to the seaside. Nobody foresaw that the Bank Holiday Act would lead to the surge of demand for holiday trips that followed. It is interesting to note that the first thing the working classes wanted to do, when faced with more time and more money, was to copy the leisure pursuits of 'their betters'. Brighton, Scarborough, Southend and other resorts were established initially to cater for the leisure demands of the landed and the wealthy. They were taken over gradually by the new emerging, but fairly rich, middle classes. By the end of the nineteenth century, it was working people that flooded into the resorts on Bank Holidays.

Government policy developed a new attitude to leisure in the mid-nineteenth century. Again quoting Coalter *et al.* (1986):

> There was also an increasing concern with the location of leisure activities and their cultural content. Here we can see the emergence of a number of themes which have, in varying degrees, remained central to public leisure policy – the physical health and moral condition of the working class, the socially integrative properties of leisure, the contribution of recreation provision to the solution of urban problems and the proper relationships between public provision and voluntary effort.
>
> (Coalter *et al.* 1986)

Local councils encouraged many leisure activities, particularly sport, by providing parks, open spaces and swimming pools. One of the problems with the move from country to town was that there was no longer any space in the new urban areas for the conventional pre-industrial popular recreations. As the nineteenth century progressed, local councils accepted the responsibility for the provision of both space and facilities for leisure in the towns and cities. In 1847, legislation was passed enabling local authorities to provide public parks. The Bank Holiday Act showed that national government would intervene to provide people with leisure time; local government set about the task of providing areas where this free time could be used 'productively'. The need for these open spaces was brought home by the 1911 census figures which showed that 80 per cent of the nation's population lived in towns and cities.

These initiatives were the first signs of government adopting a more positive role in leisure. In the past, the role of government had been to restrict leisure activities that were socially undesirable: cock-fighting, bull-baiting, dog-fighting, prostitution, gambling and drinking. In this latter half of the nineteenth century, the emphasis of government policy in leisure shifted from control and prevention (through legislation and policing) of unsocial leisure pursuits, to encouragement and support (through provision of facilities and subsidisation) of desirable recreations. A whole series of Acts appeared in the mid-nineteenth century which enabled local councils to improve the leisure opportunities for their populations: the Museums Act of 1845, the Baths and Wash-Houses Act of 1846 (leading to the provision of swimming pools) and the Public Libraries Act of 1855. It is interesting that these government initiatives were not in response to public demand; rather they were the first sign of the paternalistic role of government in encouraging leisure activities that were socially desirable. The Local Government Act of 1894 and the Open Spaces Act of 1906 allowed local councils to provide both indoor and outdoor facilities for sport and recreation. It should be emphasised though that the above-mentioned Acts were permissive rather than mandatory: local councils were not obliged to provide such leisure facilities. The Baths and Wash-Houses Act of 1846 was more concerned with public health and sanitation than with health and fitness through sport.

There is one area of sports facility provision, swimming pools, for which there is statistical evidence dating back to this period (Sports Council 1983). Although several pools and plunge baths were built in the seventeenth and eighteenth centuries (the oldest still in existence in 1977 was built in 1688), public swimming pool provision did not start to develop until after the Baths and Washhouses Act of 1846. By 1870, nearly 100 pools were in existence mostly in and around the industrial cities of Manchester, Newcastle and London. However, the real boom period in construction was between 1870 and 1900, when over 200 swimming pools were established, again mostly in and around London and Manchester but also in and around other cities in the Midlands and Yorkshire. This expansion continued into the twentieth century so that by 1914 over 500 swimming baths were open to the public in England. Thus the first major investment boom in public sector indoor sports facilities occurred between 1870 and 1914. Of these pre-1914 pools, 201 were still open in 1977.

Sports became more commercial during this period. Football had been tamed by the public schools to become an organised, respectable sport with a rigid set of rules. In 1863 the Football Association was established and the first FA Cup competition took place in 1872. The game started to attract large numbers of spectators, and football stadiums were constructed to house them. By the 1880s, professionalism in soccer was well-established. In 1895, professionalism also entered rugby when some northern clubs split away from the Rugby Union to form the new Rugby League because they wanted to remunerate players (Mason 1980).

The nineteenth century signalled the beginning of a new, more positive attitude in government policy towards sport. As Coalter *et al.* (1986) point out, there was an emphasis on improving the public provision of sport and recreation facilities as a means of improving the quality of life in urban areas. Sport and exercise were also encouraged because of concerns about the physical health of the population (and hence about its ability to fight wars).

It was during this period, the late nineteenth century, that national governing bodies (NGBs) were increasingly established in England to regulate sports and competitions nationally. It was also during this period that we saw the emergence of the first international governing bodies of sport (see Chapter 3).

It is generally acknowledged that the emergence and diffusion of modern sports on a global scale is closely connected to broader globalisation processes which took place from the 1870s to the 1920s. This period marked a decisive transformation in the spread of the old, the invention of the new and the institutionalisation of most sports on a national and even international stage.

Many of the basic ingredients of today's global sport market were therefore in place around one hundred years ago. National and international governing bodies had been set up. International sporting events had begun with four Olympiads being held before the First World War. Some ingredients were missing though, in particular broadcasting, global sports corporations and sponsorship. The whole of the period from 1914 to the present saw the increasing commercialisation of sport and the rise in economic significance of the sport market both nationally for developed countries and internationally. Broadcasting was developed relatively early in this period but the significance of global sports corporations and sponsorship are much more recent developments. The next chapter will chronicle the move to the global sport market of today.

2

THE GLOBAL SPORT MARKET

This chapter analyses the increasing economic importance of sport and the emergence of what is now recognised as a global sports industry. It begins by analysing the development of the global sport market throughout the twentieth and early twenty-first centuries. It then goes on to look at how the economics of sport developed simultaneously alongside the increasing economic importance of sport and how economics can be used to understand the global sport market.

The development of the global sport market

We have seen that even before the First World War some of the basic ingredients of the global sport market were already in place. Three elements, however, were missing: sports broadcasting, sponsorship and transnational corporations in sport. The whole of the period from 1914 to the present saw the increasing commercialisation of sport and the rise in economic significance of the sport market both nationally for developed countries and internationally. Broadcasting was developed relatively early in this period but the significance of global sports corporations and sponsorship are much more recent developments.

It is recognised that the commercialisation of sport has been apparent since the birth of modern sport, as 'the early modern sports promoters of boxing and horseracing, and later ones of baseball, football, and soccer learned readily that people would pay to see a performance' (McComb 2004). The modern Olympics were, from their inception, vulnerable to the influence of commercial forces, and some cite the inclusion of advertisements in the official programme for the first modern Games in Athens as the first sign of commercial sponsorship in sports. Tomlinson (2005) argued that 'the modern Olympics, generally, have always been commodified, in that entrance fees were set and products were put on display'. But these were modest levels of commercialisation, based upon non-profit-making and 'break-even' budgets.

Despite such an early start, economic or commercial factors did not become dominant in sport until the last quarter of the twentieth century. It is the development of global sports broadcasting and the formation of the sport–media–business nexus that has had a decisive impact on the nature of sport, changing its purpose, way of production, organisation and consumption.

Media have had a long history of association with sport, as newspapers and sports papers first brought reports to a curious public as early as the nineteenth century. Media and sport seem to be natural partners as sports stories attract sports fans and help to popularise sports and sports events, and as a result increase media sales.

Holt (1989) indicates that there has always been a strong relationship between sport and broadcasting in England:

> In fact, broadcasting first through radio and then even more dramatically on television, has been the single most important influence on the development of sport in this century. The number of radio licences rose from two to eight million between 1926 and 1939 with 71 per cent of all households having a wireless by the Second World War. The first sports broadcast, ironically at the suggestion of the *Daily Mail*, was a fight between Kid Lewis and Georges Carpentier in 1922. Sport came to have an important place in the BBC canon of 'good' entertainment, though boxing did not meet with full official approval. The aim of the new Director-General was to promote sport as well as Christianity. Reith was the true successor of the Victorian headmaster, rapidly establishing a range of sporting events which the BBC in its capacity as the sole arbiter of airways deemed to be of *national* significance. A few big events joined the list of approved patriotic 'moments' like Remembrance Day – the Wembley crowd even sang 'Abide with me' – and in Reith's words permitted the British people to be 'present equally at functions and ceremonials upon which national sentiment is consecrated'. Test cricket, rugby internationals, the Derby, and the Cup Final were established favourites. The annual rowing contest between the two ancient universities was a great London event with many ordinary families taking sides and wearing favours but it was hardly a matter of 'national' concern until the BBC included the Boat Race in the select band of truly British events. 'Look how that's come to the fore,' remarked a Bristol listener, 'we never used to know anything about it and now there's many wouldn't miss it'. Seventy per cent of the audience panel of a BBC survey in 1939 listened to the Boat Race followed by 51 per cent for boxing, 50 per cent for soccer, and 50 per cent for cricket; soccer and boxing were predictably the favourites of the working-class respondents but the 34 per cent overall interest in Wimbledon was a clear indication that hitherto bourgeois sports were broadening their appeal.
>
> (Holt 1989)

The first television sports broadcast in Britain was in 1937 when 25 minutes of a men's singles match at Wimbledon was televised. The BBC televised the international match between England and Scotland on 9 April 1938, the world's first live television pictures of a soccer match, less than a year after the Wimbledon broadcast in June 1937. A few weeks later, the BBC televised for the first time the FA Cup Final on 30 April between Huddersfield Town and Preston North End (Barnett 1990).

However, although these events were pioneering in broadcasting terms, so few people owned a television set that they made little impact on the country as a whole. As Holt (1989) comments: 'In the early 1950s no more than 10 per cent of households had a television. By the late 1960s only 10 per cent did not.'

While both print media and radio had an important impact on sport, it is the emergence of television, especially the development of satellite television, that has radically transformed it. Before that, cinema newsreels were the only way, other than attending the event, that people could observe sport performance (Whannel 2005). It is said that the first televised sporting event in the United States was a baseball game in New York City between Princeton and Columbia universities in May 1939, and there were only 400 television receivers in the city (McComb 2004).

The impact of television on sport began to become striking in the 1960s with the growing ownership of television sets. While only about 9 per cent of Americans owned a television set in 1950, the figure rose to 65 per cent in 1955, and in 1965 it had already reached 93 per cent (McComb 2004).

The development of television technology and its spread across the globe changed the nature of sports production and consumption and hence the economics of sport. The FIFA World Cup was televised for the first time in 1954, and the Rome Olympics in 1960 were the first to take advantage of the 'Eurovision link' to broadcast live around Europe (Whannel 2005). Television broadcasting has significantly increased the global popularity of both events, and contributed significantly to globalisation of sport in general. Research conducted by Sport Marketing Surveys on behalf of the IOC revealed that the Athens 2004 Summer Games achieved a record television audience of 3.9 billion globally, compared with 3.6 billion for the 2000 Sydney Games. The cumulative TV audience estimate was 40 billion, and there were 35,000 hours of coverage of the Athens Games compared with 29,600 for Sydney, and 20,000 for Barcelona (1992) (Olympic.org 2009).

Described by FIFA as 'the world's No. 1 sports event', the 2006 FIFA World Cup Germany is said to have had a total cumulative television audience of 26.29 billion (24.2 billion in-home and 2.1 billion out-of-home viewers). FIFA's research also indicated that the 2006 event was aired in a total of 43,600 broadcasts across 214 countries and territories, generating total coverage of 73,072 hours, an increase of 76 per cent on the 2002 event (41,435 hours) and a 148 per cent increase on 1998 (FIFA 2007).

Television does far more than merely relay major sports events to the audience, as it radically re-constructs them, combining live and recorded 'feeds' from venue and studio, adding replay, slow-motion, montage, commentary and discussion (Whannel 2005). Whannel (2005) argued that within a television landscape where much is recorded, safe and predictable, only news and sport offer uncertainty, risk and 'liveness', and a powerful sense of being there as it happens. Roone Arledge, the director of ABC sports, made similar comments about the attraction of sport as he wrote the famous lines repeated at the introduction of every edition of *Wide World of Sports* (1961–98), 'Spanning the globe to bring you the constant variety of sport, the thrill of victory, the agony of defeat, the human drama of athletic competition' (McComb 2004).

This attraction of television sports has turned major live sporting events transmitted around the world into a key element in broadcast schedules and the media industry (Whannel 2005). The economic relationship has to be understood by looking at the nature of television sport consumption: watching television involves opportunity cost, and a financial transaction occurs within the distribution channel through the sale of advertising directed at the fan or the witnessing of sponsorship images even if the consumer is watching a free-to-air sports event (Forster and Pope 2004). Such components of the market constitute the non-core product of sport and it is this element that forms the basis of the relationship between sport and TV (Forster and Pope 2004). As a result, television sport did not only help to launch the TV industry, but has also shaped the industry structure. ABC created the first network sports division in the USA in 1959. In 1960, ABC was third in the ratings, and by 1976 it was first. This was done in partnership with Gillette who gave US$8.5 million in TV advertising during sports programmes. Another example of the powerful effect of TV sport is Super Bowl games. They are the biggest single event in US sport, and by 1991, a 30-second spot in the telecast cost US$875,000 (Forster and Pope 2004). In 2011 the cost of a 30-second advertising slot had risen to $3 million.

The television industry has to rely on high viewing rates to obtain advertising revenue. The potential for huge audiences, even during the day and late at night, and usually during the slack summer season as is the case of the summer Olympic Games, has led to growing competition between television networks for exclusive broadcasting rights for major sports events (Whannel 2005).

This competition brings significant sums of money into sports and helps to transform the economics of global sports and sports events. Broadcasting rights fees have become a major, sometimes predominant, source of revenue for sports. In the case of the Olympic Games, TV rights accounted for 53 per cent (US$2.229 billion) of total revenue, followed by sponsorship (34 per cent, US$1.459 billion), and ticketing (11 per cent, US$441 million) for the period 2001–4 (Horne and Manzenreiter 2007). The explosive growth of television sport and the huge sums of money generated by broadcasting rights fees has changed the economics of sport, turning it into a highly commercialised commodity. Sponsorship has had a similar effect.

Popular sporting events that can attract a global audience via broadcasting become ideal vehicles for corporate sponsors seeking to raise the global profile of their brands. Such events 'transcend cultural differences and, being universal in appeal, open up access to consumer markets around the world in a way that few other social and cultural practices can equal' (Smart 2007). As such, they offer multinational corporations a unique platform for brand building and global marketing.

One of the earliest recorded event sponsorships in modern sport was that of the England cricket team's 1861 tour of Australia by catering company Spiers and Pond (Gratton and Taylor 2000). The inclusion of advertisements in the official programme for the first modern Olympics in Athens is another example of early sports sponsorship.

Despite such an early start, it has only been in the last quarter of the twentieth century, in association with developments in sports television broadcasting, that corporate sponsorship began to have a marked impact on sports.

From the late 1970s and early 1980s, corporate sponsorship of global sports events began to grow dramatically. FIFA 'was the first global sports organisation for which corporate sponsorship became a major source of revenue generation, with the World Cup becoming the main tournament for securing lucrative global commercial sponsorship agreements and for auctioning the sale of global television broadcasting rights' (Smart 2007). Horne and Manzenreiter (2007) argue that the idea of selling exclusive marketing rights to a limited number of sponsors to increase revenue first began in Britain in the 1970s with Patrick Nally and his associate, Peter West, as the media agency WestNally. The idea was taken up by Horst Dassler, son of the founder of shoe manufacturing company Adidas, when he worked with FIFA and its president, Havelange, to establish exclusive marketing rights agreements with major global corporations for the World Cup tournament. They began with the 1978 World Cup in Argentina, for which contracts were negotiated with six major corporate sponsors, including Coca-Cola and Gillette, which established a template that would be followed in subsequent tournaments.

It is generally recognised that the 1984 Los Angeles Olympics was a watershed in the commercialisation of the Olympic Games and providing a model in financing major events in general. Until 1984, global sporting events such as the Olympics were increasingly regarded as a financial burden to organisers. It was Peter Ueberroth, the head of Los Angeles Olympic Organizing Committee, who made history. Unlike organisers of Montreal's 1976 Olympics who had sold sponsorship rights to 628 'official' partners, Ueberroth drastically reduced the number of sponsors to 34 but managed to increase the price to an unprecedented $4 million minimum per corporation. The total sponsorship and licensing revenue reached a record high of US$126.7 million, compared to US$7 million at the 1976 Games. Ueberroth showed how establishing a limited number of product categories and guaranteeing exclusive sponsorships in each category could trigger bidding wars between rival companies and thus maximise sponsorship revenue. The 1984 Games is described as inaugurating the most successful era of corporate sponsorship in Olympic history.

Commercialisation and globalisation, prompted by global television media and multinational corporations (MNCs), have radically transformed the nature of modern sport, turning it from an amateur-based pastime into a serious multi-billion-dollar global business and established industry. As this emerging global sports industry has grown astronomically in economic terms over the last 40 to 50 years, so has the interest of sport economists.

The economics of sport

The first articles on the subject of sport economics appeared in the 1950s and 1960s with Rottenberg's (1956) article on the labour market for baseball players normally recognised as the first (Andreff and Symanski 2006). Neale's (1964) article entitled

'The peculiar economics of professional sports' highlighted the fact that applying economics to professional sport required a slightly different type of economic analysis than when applied to other areas. Most of these early articles in the economics of sport originated in North America and concerned the four main professional team sports there: American football, baseball, ice–hockey and basketball. Even now in North America, sport economics is still mainly concerned with the economics of professional team sports and not with the global developments in sport that have been described in the previous section.

In the late 1970s and early 1980s, some British economists (Sloane 1971; Bird 1982; Jennett 1984) applied the economics of professional sports to football in Britain, pointing out the differences from North America. This area of economics expanded substantially after the formation of the English Premier League in 1992 and the subsequent rapid expansion in the revenues of the clubs belonging to this league mainly through the expansion of broadcasting rights, sponsorship income and commercial income. Although this is related to the globalisation of the sport market, it was not the main area of concern of the economists working in this area at that time. The main areas of interest were uncertainty of outcome, and its relationship to match attendances, and the role of professional sports leagues in controlling competition.

A broader approach to sport economics, however, did develop in Europe mainly from the 1980s onwards that went beyond the study of the economics of professional team sports. Andreff and Symanski (2006) point to developments in France and Germany where the economics of sport was extended to all sport activities both professional and amateur. Gratton and Taylor's (1985) *Sport and Recreation: An Economic Analysis* was the first book that adopted this broader approach to sport which defined sport economics as concerned with the economic analysis of the sport market, that is the demand for and supply of sporting opportunities. Many European countries (e.g. the Netherlands, the UK, Belgium, Finland, Denmark, France and Germany) carried out studies of the economic importance of sport in the 1980s with some of these countries having repeated the exercise in the 1990s. Jones (1989) reviewed the entire first round of European economic impact of sport studies and Andreff (1994) reviewed developments in the early 1990s.

These and subsequent studies have shown that sport is an important sector of economic activity accounting for close to 2 per cent of both Gross Domestic Product (GDP) and employment. Despite recent focus on the amount of money involved in sport at the elite level in terms of sponsorship, payments of broadcasting rights, transfer fees and players' salaries, in fact consumer expenditure on sport is not dominated by payments related to major professional sports. Instead, consumer expenditure in the sport market consists in the main of expenditure related to the consumer's own participation in sport rather than as a spectator. By far the largest sector of the sport market consists of all the products which are bought for use in sport, such as sports clothing and footwear, equipment, and services such as subscription fees to sports clubs and entry charges to sports facilities.

Figure 2.1 shows the hierarchical nature of the sport market with a relatively small group of elite athletes at the top of the pyramid competing in national and

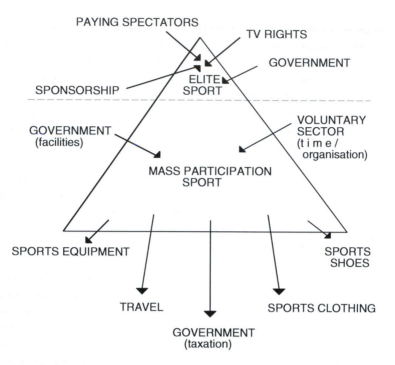

FIGURE 2.1 The sport market

international competitions. At this top level of sport money flows into sport from sponsorship, from paying spectators, and from television companies eager to broadcast this high standard of competition.

Although this elite end of the sport market appears to be essentially commercial, it is also subsidised by government. Economics can help to both provide a rationale for and assess the cost effectiveness of such a subsidy. Every country would like to see its own sportsmen and sportswomen as international champions. There is a national demand in every country for international sporting success. Governments fund the top end of the sport market in order to 'produce' sporting excellence and international sporting success both through their own direct expenditure and through their control of sports funds through government agencies.

At the bottom of the pyramid is recreational sport: people taking part in sport for fun, for enjoyment or maybe in order to get fitter and healthier. This part is also subsidised by government but predominantly by local government through subsidies to sports facilities in the community and in schools. Again, economic analysis explores both the rationale and the efficiency of such government intervention. Government subsidies at this level are much higher than those directed at the elite end of the sport market. Figure 2.1 also identifies another important source of resources into sport, the voluntary sector. The resources the voluntary sector contributes to sport are massive, but the most important resource is the time that volunteers contribute to sport without payment and it is not an easy task putting a monetary valuation on this.

Although government and the voluntary sector support the recreational end of the sport market, there are substantial monetary flows from sports participants to the commercial sector through their expenditures on sports equipment, clothes, and shoes. These same participants also contribute to government revenue in the form of taxation on sport-related expenditures and incomes. In fact, in most developed countries the amount that sports participants give back to the government in taxation through expenditures on their sport participation is greater than the amount of government subsidies to sport. Sport gives more back to government than government gives to sport.

One final important area that is only just starting to be recognised and quantified as a sport-related expenditure is sport-related travel. Leisure travel is an important part of travel expenditure, accounting for over 30 per cent of all travel expenditure in many developed countries. Sport-related travel has increased its share of all leisure travel consistently over the last 20 years so that it now accounts for about 10 per cent of all leisure travel in the UK.

Figure 2.1 indicates the complex nature of the sport market. The supply side of the sport market is a mixture of three types of provider: the public sector, the voluntary sector and the commercial sector. Government supports sport both to promote mass participation and to generate excellence, but government also imposes taxation on sport. The commercial sector sponsors sport both at the elite level and at the grass roots. Some of these sponsors (e.g. Nike, Adidas and Reebok) do so in order to promote their sports products and receive a return on this sponsorship through expenditure by sports participants on their products. Most of sports sponsorship is, however, from the non-sports commercial sector (e.g. Coca-Cola, McDonalds), where the motives for the sponsorship are less directly involved with selling a product to sports participants. Squeezed in between government and the commercial sector is the voluntary sector, putting resources into sport mainly through the contribution of free labour time, but needing also to raise enough revenue to cover costs since the voluntary sector cannot raise revenue through taxation as government can.

If the supply side of the sport market is complicated, then so is the demand side. The demand for sport is a composite demand involving the demand for free time; the demand to take part in sport; the demand for equipment, shoes, and clothing; the demand for facilities; and the demand for travel. Taking part in sport involves, therefore, the generation of demand for a range of goods and services which themselves will be provided by the mixture of public, commercial and voluntary organisations discussed above.

To this complexity of the demand to take part in sport, can be added the complication that the sport market is a mixture of both participant demands and spectator demands of different types. As we move up the hierarchy towards elite sport, there is an increasing demand to watch sporting competitions. Some of these spectators may also take part but many do not. The spectators may go to a specific sports event, or watch at a distance on television. Alternatively, they may not 'watch' at all, preferring to listen on the radio or read about it in newspapers. All of these activities are part of the demand side of the sport market.

In fact, market demand is even more complicated than this rather complex picture since Figure 2.1 only represents the flows into and out of a national sport market. Increasingly it is more appropriate to talk about the global sport market. A small, but increasing, part of every country's sport market is international or global. There already exist sporting competitions that are of truly global dimensions: over two thirds of the world's population (over 4 billion people) watch some part of the global television coverage of the Olympic Games. The cumulative television audience for the football World Cup is normally over 40 billion. Equally there are commercial companies that produce, distribute, and market their product on a global basis. Nike designs its sports shoes in Oregon, USA, contracts out the production of these shoes to factories in Thailand, Indonesia, China and Korea, and markets the shoes on a global basis using a symbol (the swoosh) and, in the past, three words that were understood throughout the world ('Just Do It'). Nike, in 1997, rose to one hundred and sixty-seventh in the world's Top 500 companies with a market capitalisation of $17.5 billion.

Although the main process of globalisation takes place at the elite end of the sport market, the bottom end of the market is provided for by global sports corporations such as Nike and Adidas, who provide the shoes, clothing and equipment that make up the largest share of the sport market. The economics of sport used to treat the sport market as a national market, looking at the demand side and the supply side of the market and analysing the main factors affecting each. Although this approach is still relevant to some extent, increasingly it is more appropriate to talk about the global sport market. As Maguire et al. (2002) point out: 'dominant, emergent, and residual patterns of sport and leisure practices are closely intertwined with the globalisation process'. An increasing and hugely important part of every country's sport market is international or global. The major globalising forces are: the increasing globalisation of media coverage of major sports events (e.g. the Olympics, the World Cup); the creation of new global sports events (e.g. the Cricket World Cup, the Rugby World Cup) driven by the eagerness of global sports organisations to promote their sport; global television coverage of what were formerly domestic events (e.g. English Premier League); global recognition of the top athletes competing in these events; and association of these athletes with global sports brands (e.g. Nike, Adidas). The characteristics of the global sport market that emerged were: escalation in the price of broadcasting rights to the top sports events; global marketing of major sports products by using images (not words) recognisable worldwide; sports celebrities becoming the most important part of these images; escalation in the price of sponsorship deals for both events and athletes by both sport (e.g. Nike, Adidas) and non-sport (e.g. Coca-Cola, McDonalds) sponsors.

To understand the economics of the modern global sport market we need to understand the behaviour of the main global sports organisations, the influence of the major sports events these organisations own, the role of global sports corporations, and of the main global sports sponsors. Finally we need to understand the economics of the sports broadcasting market. These topics form the chapters in the rest of the book.

3

GLOBAL SPORTS ORGANISATIONS

Introduction

Chapter 1 indicated that National Governing Bodies (NGBs) emerged in the nineteenth century to organise the newly formalised sports. As these sports increasingly looked for international competition, the NGBs got together to set up international governing bodies in the various sports. Thus, initially, most of these international governing bodies were the creation of their national equivalents and were controlled by them. The international governing bodies were an umbrella body of national associations. In economic terms, they were voluntary sector non-profit organisations as were the NGBs. In the early years many were more like gentlemen's clubs and most were dominated by the English since England's NGBs were the oldest and strongest.

These early international governing bodies bore little resemblance to the Global Sports Organisations (GSOs) such as the Fédération Internationale de Football Association (FIFA) and the International Olympic Committee (IOC) that we see today. Forster and Pope (2004) argue that these GSOs have the 'ability to shape not only sports culture but also the sports economy, its markets, consumers, and producers'. They go on to point out that the GSOs 'have been and remain the most influential instruments in the creation of sport as a global cultural phenomenon'.

The aim of this chapter is to understand how these GSOs have acquired such a powerful position in the global sport market and to analyse in detail how they exercise this power.

Emergence of national sports organisations

It is clear that codified and standardised rules are crucial in the development of modern sport. NGBs played a key role in this formalisation process. These organisations have been instrumental and essential in codification of rules, setting schedules, organising competitions and overseeing officiating at matches. This is probably why bureaucratic organisation is viewed by some (e.g. Craig 2002) as the most important of all characteristics of modern sport. It is worth noting that codification, the creation of explicit codes of rules, is only one of the first steps in the overall formalisation of sport, and this process often had begun before the NGBs were formed. Yet as a sport develops, some formal organisation is required to maintain and modify the rules as well as coordinate and organise competitions between interested parties who wish to play the sport by these rules. As Forster and Pope (2004) argued, the prior creation of codes, and the competitions and events using those codes, became the catalyst for the creation of sports organisations. In the language of rational choice and liberal institutionalism, these organisations helped to reduce transaction costs, facilitate information exchange and provide focal points for interested parties for cooperation and coordination.

This rational choice approach is very convincing in terms of explaining the demand for sports organisations and why they were established, but it will not tell us much about how and when these organisations would be established. Actually, there have been dramatic differences in the way that sports organisations developed, and to a certain degree, sports have been formalised at a very different pace, each with a unique evolutionary history.

NGBs were increasingly established in the mid- to late nineteenth century in England to regulate sports and competitions nationally. The impulse to formalise and organise the activities swept through British society in a wave: the Football Association in 1863; the Bicycle Union in 1866; the Amateur Swimming Association in 1869, and the handling version of football became organised under the Rugby Football Union in 1871. Major Wingfield published and subsequently marketed the rules of lawn tennis in 1874. The Hockey Association followed in 1876 and the Amateur Rowing Association in 1882. Table 3.1 shows the foundation years for some of the early English sports governing bodies across a range of modern sports.

TABLE 3.1 Foundation years of early English national governing bodies and international federations

Sport	National Association	Year	International Federation	Year
Football	FA	1863	FIFA	1904
Bicycle	BU	1866	UCI	1900
Swimming	ASA	1869	IRB	1886
Rugby	RFU	1871	ISU	1892
Ice skating	NSAGB	1879	IAAF	1912
Athletics	AAA	1880	IBU professional	1911
			FIBA amateurs	1920
Boxing	ABA	1880	FISA	1892
Rowing	ARA	1882	FINA	1908
Gymnastics	AGA	1888	FIG	1881
Lawn tennis	LTA	1888	ILTF	1913
Badminton	BE	1893	BWF	1934
Fencing	AFA	1902	FIE	1913

Source: Scambler (2005: 44); Craig (2002: 58), and IOC website (2010)

With the intensification of globalisation partly driven by industrialisation and technological advancement, English sport and its organisational forms diffused to Europe, the USA and the British Empire, and then to the rest of the world. In the main, the way of organising sport followed the general model whereby 'a voluntary organisation, essentially a collection of voluntary sports clubs, set themselves up as the national governing body for their sport in that country'(Wolsey and Abrams 2001). Naturally, international competitions, tournaments and tours began to occur with increasing frequency. These included the first international rugby and football matches between Scotland and England held in Edinburgh (1871) and Glasgow (1872) respectively, the first cricket test match between Australia and England (1877), the first international team tennis competition, later known as the Davis Cup in 1900, and the first England international football team tour to continental Europe in 1908 (Smart 2007; Wolsey and Abrams 2001).

Increasingly, international governing bodies of sport (IGBs), also known as international federations (IFs) in the Olympic Movement, were founded to govern sports and competitions across borders. The Federation of International Gymnastics was founded in 1881, making it the oldest international sports federation. The International Olympic Committee (IOC), arguably the most powerful and influential sports organisation in the world, was founded in 1894. The Fédération Internationale de Football Association (FIFA) was formed in 1904; the International Amateur Athletic Federation in 1912; the Fédération Internationale de Natation (FINA) in 1908; and the International Tennis Federation (ITF) in 1913. By 1920, half of the current Olympic Sports (for the 2016 Games) had their respective international federations established. Once established, these GSOs often sought to promote their sport and games across the globe at both elite level and in participation.

GSOs

GSOs are international NGOs that govern sports and/or global sporting events. According to Forster and Pope (2004) there are at least three types of sports organisations that fall into this category.

The first type, and the vast majority of GSOs, are international governing bodies of sports (IGBs). For many sports, there is one recognised international governing body for the sport, and this one body is responsible for the development and control of that sport including its rules of competition. This control is exercised and maintained via membership whereby all those who wish to participate in a sport are governed by the rules and conditions of that body (Masterman 2004). For example, the Fédération Internationale de Football Association (FIFA) and the International Association of Athletic Federations (IAAF) govern the rules for football and athletics respectively on a global basis. Collectively, these governing bodies are referred to as IGBs in the UK or International Federations (IFs) by the International Olympic Committee (IOC) (Masterman 2004).

The second type of GCSOs are event-orientated organisations which organise multi-sport games regularly and have a purpose other than sport. For example, the IOC has long claimed that it helped promote world peace through the Olympic Games and Olympic Movement. The Federation of Gay Games perpetuates the quadrennial Gay Games and safeguards its founding principles of participation, inclusion and personal best (FGG 2009). The International University Sports Federation (FISU) has organised World Student Games regularly since 1924.

The third type are function-orientated specialists. These GSOs are concerned with technical issues of sports medicine, the law and quasi-legal issues, adjudication, arbitration, doping and the use of performance drugs, and other technological developments increasingly affecting sport. For example, the World Anti-Doping Agency (WADA) was established in 1999 as an international independent agency composed and funded equally by the sports movement and governments of the world. Its key activities include scientific research, education, development of anti-doping capacities, and monitoring of the World Anti-Doping Code ('The Code') – the document standardising anti-doping policies in all sports and all countries (WADA 2009). It is argued that the reasons for the emergence of these specialist GSOs are: the requirement for the independence of some of the functions that they perform from the individual sporting bodies; the economies of specialisation; and the interests of client GSOs in divorcing themselves from some of the activities that may cause conflict between subordinate international federations and themselves (Forster and Pope 2004).

The emergence of GSOs can also be understood as part of a wider movement towards a global civil society in response to the need for global governance. Globalisation is generally understood as a process that involves world economy, politics and culture becoming increasingly interconnected and interdependent. Globalisation is nothing new, and different historical forms of globalisation are characterised by distinctive spatio-temporal and organisational attributes (Held and McGrew 2002). Contemporary globalisation distinguished itself from earlier periods with growing intensification both in scope and degree, creating a world in which the extensive reach of global relations and networks is matched by their relative high intensity, high velocity, and high impact propensity across many facets of social life, from the political, and economic to the environmental and cultural (Keohane and Nye 2000; Held and McGrew 2002).

A natural but critical question is: how can this globalisation be governed in a world with growing complexities and uncertainties but without a world government?

Globalisation calls for global governance that requires international coordination and cooperation across borders. According to Keohane and Nye (2000), global governance can be regarded as global processes and institutions, both formal and informal, that guide and restrain the collective activities of actors of various kinds and at various levels.

While governments are still essential in this process, non-state actors are now playing an increasingly important role. As Rosenau (1992) pointed out, a complex multi-centric world consisting of diverse and relatively autonomous actors is emerging, and this world is expected to be shaped in part by a number of non-state players including multinational corporations (MNCs), ethnic minorities, sub-national governments and bureaucracies, professional societies.

International Non-Government Organisations (INGOs), one of the fastest-growing non-state actors over the last few decades, are playing an increasingly active and influential role in constructing a new international culture, shaping people's ideas about a fast-changing and inter-linked world. Whereas up to 1854, only six INGOs had been founded, by the end of the nineteenth century this figure had reached 163, and by 2007 it was claimed that there were over 60,000 INGOs in the world (Davies 2008). More and more people see the growth of INGOs both in numbers and influence as the emergence of a transnational or even global civil society (Wild 2006).

These INGOs sometimes cooperate, and at other times they compete, but essentially they interact and intertwine with state and other non-state actors in this process of culture construction and rule making. In some situations, INGOs can be even more competent and effective than governments (Liu 2004).

So the birth of GSOs can be understood as part of this broader movement of global civil society, as many of them were among the first of the INGOs to be founded as a coherent group (Forster and Pope 2004). They share two basic features in common with other INGOs: non-governmental and not-for-profit. Unlike government agencies, they cannot rely on public funding or legal authority, but operate essentially as part of the voluntary sector just like NGOs. They are also different from multinational corporations as their major objective is not to make a profit. Many GSOs do engage in activities that generate profits but these activities are considered to be only secondary, aimed at fundraising in order to pursue their primary sporting objectives.

INGOs are often committed to a mission that seeks to attract their constituency by claiming high moral grounds and holding universal values that transcend state borders, nationalities, classes, cultures, and races. In contrast, actors such as governments and business are often regarded as self-interested power- or profit-seekers. It is argued that INGOs' universal value claims and multi-perspective approaches, which tend to transcend international, cultural, and racial boundaries, may help to cultivate and increase a community among its constituencies across the globe.

Those universal principles, norms, and values held, advocated, and promoted by INGOs may contribute to the formation of this global citizenship in that they first of all raise the awareness of an international community across borders. INGOs' international programmes and networks also provide a tangible platform and space to act on this new identity (Liu 2004).

The modern Olympic Movement can be cited as a good example that fitted well with this global civil society movement, as De Coubertin's conception and creation of the Olympics in 1894 was internationalist in purpose and the IOC has long portrayed itself as a force for world peace (Forster and Pope 2004). In other words, sport and the Games were seen as a means to this internationalist end, rather than the event being an end in itself (Forster and Pope 2004). Many other GSOs have adopted this internationalist position as a tool for achieving broader acceptance and legitimacy. Their original *raison d'être* may have been sport, but other broader societal objectives were incorporated.

Theoretical issues

National Governing Bodies of sport are normally treated in economics as part of the voluntary non-profit sector (Gratton and Taylor 2000) and therefore we would expect GSOs to be categorised in the same way. One economist, Weisbrod, has developed a theory of the voluntary non-profit sector and this approach has been used by Gratton and Taylor (1991) to apply that theory to the voluntary sector in sport. Weisbrod (1978, 1988) provided an economic rationale for the existence of the voluntary sector. He saw it as essentially fulfilling the same role as government, providing collective goods, but in a special set of market circumstances.

Economic welfare principles provide us with reasons for government intervention in the sport market. When a private market operates successfully, but still it fails to cater adequately for the full effects of the market on the welfare of society, economists call this a 'market failure' situation. There are several causes of market failure which are relevant to the market for sport. In each case the existence of market failure is in principle a reason for government intervention, since intervention has the potential to prevent or compensate for the market failure (Gratton and Taylor 2000). As examples here we use the relationship between sport and health and the public good nature of international sporting success.

As Gratton (2004) argued, it is now generally accepted that sport and physical activity can have an important positive impact on health. In particular:

- Regular physical activity decreases the risk of cardiovascular mortality in general and of coronary heart disease mortality in particular.
- Regular physical activity prevents or delays the development of high blood pressure, and reduces blood pressure in people with hypertension.
- Physical activity is also important in helping people to control their body weight, and in controlling diabetes.
- Specific forms of physical activity can help to reduce the risk of falls and accidents, by improving bone health and maintaining strength, coordination, cognitive functioning and balance.
- Physical activity reduces the risk of colon cancer, and evidence is growing to support links with other forms of cancer. Moderately intense physical activity enhances the immune system.
- Physical activity reduces the risk of depression, and has positive benefits for mental health including reducing anxiety, and enhancing mood and self-esteem.
- Physical activity can play a valuable role in the prevention and treatment of non-specific chronic low back pain.

There is evidence to suggest that a more efficient means of achieving health policy objectives may be to redistribute resources from health services to direct expenditure on the provision or subsidisation of active recreation services in order to improve the health of the population. The relationship between sport and health is not the only market failure to support the argument for government intervention in the sport market but it is one of its strongest arguments.

A rather different argument relates to government intervention in elite sport in order to generate international sporting success. Gratton and Taylor (2000) argue that international sporting success is a public good (also referred to as 'collective goods').

The principal characteristics attached to such goods are that they are non-rival and non-excludable in consumption. Non-rival means that one person's consumption does not prevent another person from enjoying exactly the same product at the same time. Non-excludable means that no consumer can be prevented from enjoying the product. Under these two conditions, private market provision is not worthwhile, so public goods will be underprovided by the private market.

Because many of the benefits of international sporting success (e.g. improved national morale, increased interest in sport) are such that nobody can be prevented from feeling them, they are non-excludable. Because everyone can enjoy these benefits together with no congestion in consumption, they are non-rival. A free market would underprovide such public goods, because there is always the temptation for consumers to become 'free riders', benefiting from the products without paying for them. Governments can ensure that adequate provision is made for excellence in sport to be produced, and also ensure that those who benefit from this public good pay, through taxes.

These are only two examples of market failure in the sport market and we do see government intervention in the sport market in many countries both to encourage more sports participation for health reasons and to support elite sport, in particular Olympic sports since many countries now have elite sports strategies aiming to maximise success at the Olympics. However, according to Weisbrod, governments fail to correct for all private market failures. In other words, a combination of commercial market failure and government failure leaves opportunities for a third major provider, the non-profit supplier.

Weisbrod argued that two reasons are particularly relevant to the stimulation of voluntary-sector activity. Government itself lacks adequate information on consumer demands and also government officials often follow their own personal objectives rather than acting on the basis of abstract concepts of market efficiency. Government may be an efficient provider of collective goods if demand for such goods is homogeneous. In circumstances where there are diverse demands, the voluntary sector is likely to be the more efficient provider:

> When a collective good is collective for only some persons – in the sense that the good enters positively the utility functions of only those persons – the potential for organising collective good activity outside of government, in voluntary non-profit organisations, appears more likely.
>
> (Weisbrod 1978)

In effect, Weisbrod suggests that there has to be a wide degree of consensus on the collective nature of a good before government enters the market. For minority interests government is likely to fail to provide collective benefits:

> The undersatisfied demand for collective type goods is a government 'failure' analogous to private market failure. That is, the combined willingness of part of the population to pay for additional collective-type goods exceeds the

incremental cost of providing them and yet government, responding to majoritarian interests, does not provide them.

(Weisbrod 1988)

Government fails to obtain relevant information on consumer demand when demand is heterogeneous and fragmented, even when the nature of the good concerned is collective. There are several reasons for this.

First, there is a motivation problem. The behaviourist model indicates that politicians are likely to be more concerned with the objective of maximising their chances of re-election than meeting an abstract social welfare objective. Where there is a majority demand for a collective good, then the two objectives are likely to lead to the same action, provision of the good. However, for minority interest collective goods, the re-election objective is not necessarily fulfilled by provision.

Second, there is an information problem. For majority interests, there is less likely to be a problem in politicians perceiving the demand for the collective good. For minority interests, it is much more difficult to establish the strength of demand.

Added to this are the inefficiencies in the implementation of the decisions of the politician through the bureaucratic process. It is perhaps not surprising that there is a significant part of consumer demand for collective goods that goes unmet by both the commercial sector and government. The voluntary sector fills the gap.

Weisbrod's argument is specifically relevant to sport because the nature of the demand for sport is such that demand is likely to be fragmented. Data on participation rates shows that demand for any particular sport is a minority demand. The fragmentation of NGBs in sport is partly a reflection of different interests within individual sports. At the same time, participation in sport is a collective good in the sense that there are presumed societal benefits over and above benefits to individual participants such as sports contribution to health. The sports club, therefore, in Weisbrod's terms, arises out of the failure of both markets and government to provide for a heterogeneous demand for sport. Markets fail to provide sufficiently because of the collective nature of the good; governments fail because of the heterogeneous nature of demand.

Weisbrod discussed the wide spectrum of types of non-profit organisation. At one end are organisations almost entirely dependent on income from members, i.e. clubs. Buchanan (1965) analysed the economic formation of clubs. The benefits of such organisations accrue only to the members of the club; in fact, Buchanan saw the objective of such a club as the maximisation of the net benefit of the typical member. The good provided is collective in a sense, but it is excludable and is made exclusive to the club members.

At the other end of the spectrum 'collective-type non-profits, such as providers of medical research and aid to the poor, produce public-type services that bring widely shared benefits' (Weisbrod 1988). These organisations imitate government at a micro scale. Government does not provide such collective benefits because of their minority nature or because of information inadequacies. Such organisations are, however, likely to be publicly subsidised and receive a large part of their income in the form of contributions, gifts, or grants.

Weisbrod suggests a 'collectiveness index' to measure the percentage of an organisation's income that comes from such sources. An organisation that provides mainly private goods and services to its own members (i.e. clubs) would be expected to have a 'collectiveness index' close to zero. At the opposite extreme, any non-profit organisation providing purely collective goods (i.e. all the benefits accruing to individuals who did not pay for them) would have a collectiveness index approaching 100. Thus we have a whole variety of voluntary sector organisations.

It seems that many sports clubs (e.g. amateur football clubs, athletics clubs, etc.) would be at the 'private good' end of Weisbrod's spectrum of voluntary sector organisations. Weisbrod argued that this type of non-profit is most similar to the commercial sector. Most of the income comes from membership fees and from sales. There is little or no public subsidy since few if any benefits are generated for non-members: the collectiveness index therefore should be very low.

In many countries, the majority of sports club income comes from two sources: membership subscriptions and fees, and bar profits. The next largest source of income is from raffles, gaming and other fundraising activities. Since it is normally the members themselves who drink in the club bar and use the gaming machines, the majority of the income from sports clubs comes from members.

If we consider the typical amateur sports club, then the picture is quite clear. The benefits provided by the club are exclusive to its members. Their participation in their chosen sport is made easier and considerably cheaper by the organisation provided mainly by voluntary labour. Although there is an element of altruistic giving in the volunteer labour provided to sports clubs, most of this labour is provided by the players themselves (the main beneficiaries), former players (and hence former beneficiaries), relatives of the players (hence indirect consumers of the benefits), or volunteers who receive positive utility through their involvement in the sport.

Thus, the product provided by the typical sports club is essentially a private product. People participate in the club for reasons of self-interest rather than altruism. The motivation of club members is not to generate collective benefits of sport for society generally but rather to maximise benefits for club members. The fact that some collective benefits are incidentally generated may mean that the club is treated favourably by government (e.g. grants, subsidised charges for facilities or ground rental), but this is not normally the case.

We have seen earlier in this chapter that the formation of national sports organisations and then global sports organisations was a natural progression in the development of sport. National sports organisations were needed for the codification of rules, for setting schedules, organising competitions and overseeing officiating at matches. These organisations were providing benefits for their members, the clubs, and are clearly at the private good end of Weisbrod's spectrum. Initially, the income to national sports bodies would have come from the contributions of member clubs and/or players. Most GSOs were initially set up by the national sports organisations to organise and control international competition. They were controlled by the national sports organisations and funded from the contributions of members. Thus Weisbrod's theory of non-profits provides a model to explain the early behaviour of

GSOs and, for some of them, it still does since not all of them attract massive income from broadcasting rights and sponsorship. However, the globalisation of the sport market, particularly over the last 30 to 40 years, has made this model inappropriate for many GSOs today that have managed to substantially increase their commercial income.

From non-profit to commercialisation

As sport and mega-sporting events such as the Olympics and the FIFA World Cup evolved into part of an industry on a global scale driven by professionalisation, commercialisation and global media, these GSOs are increasingly involved in commercial and profit-making activities. Generating revenue was a tool GSOs used to achieve sporting ends. Over time though, sport has evolved within an environment that has made it the means to achieving financial ends.

Commercialisation and globalisation, prompted by global television media and multinational corporations (MNCs), have radically transformed the nature of modern sport, turning it from an amateur-based playful activity into a serious multi-billion-dollar global business and established industry. Even during a time of world economic crisis and global recession, research shows that some US$29.182 billion worth of deals have been completed across the global sports industry in the first quarter of 2009 alone, 'an extraordinary figure given the worldwide economic situation' (Fraser 2009).

This transformation of sport has had a profound impact on the purpose, role and behaviour of many GSOs. With sport turning into financially rewarding business, some GSOs, as governing bodies of sports and sports events, have become increasingly involved in marketing and profit generation and distribution activities, and have in general turned into 'business non-governmental organizations' (BNGOs).

It should be noted that the commercialisation of sport has not happened without resistance, and the transformation of GSOs is evolutionary rather than revolutionary. Very often, GSOs have been passive and have reacted to commercial influence. In many cases, GSOs have demonstrated strong scepticism and even vehement opposition toward commercialisation, before moving towards embracing it. This is best illustrated by the evolution of the Olympic movement.

De Coubertin, the founder of the modern Olympics, and several of his successors had made constant efforts to guard the Games from monetary contamination. Avery Brundage, who was the president of the IOC from 1952 to 1972, made every effort to prevent the Games from moving toward professionalisation and commercialisation. Even at the time of his retirement in 1972, Brundage was still declaring that the IOC 'should have nothing to do with money', as he believed that arguments over the distribution of money threatened to 'fracture the Olympic Movement' (Barney *et al.* 2002, cf. Tomlinson, 2005). It was not until the early 1980s, under Juan Antonio Samaranch's presidency, that the IOC abandoned amateur restrictions and voted to accept corporate sponsorship (Phillips 1999). This evolutionary process of commercialisation is also evidenced by the fact that many GSOs, such as the IAAF, still retained the word 'amateur' in their official name, even long after they abandoned the amateur rule.

On the other hand, commercialisation and globalisation do not affect all sports in the same way. While there are commercially successful sports like soccer, tennis and golf, there are also commercially less successful sports such as shooting, judo and weightlifting (Stokvis 2000). Despite this variation, no national or international sports organisations are immune to market forces and can 'afford to be indifferent to commercial sponsorship' (Stokvis 2000).

By the end of twentieth century, commercialisation of sport had become more pervasive than ever before, to the point that 'at no other historical moment have commercial or economic factors totally dominated the landscape of sports' (Berkshire Encyclopaedia of World Sports, 2005). As Whannel (2005) indicates: 'In most individual sports, the old, traditional, amateur paternalistic governing bodies have been forced to reshape themselves, ceding some of their power and privilege to the demands of the modern market-driven enterprise culture'.

With global sport turning into 'a serious and increasingly financially rewarding business' (Smart 2007), the behaviour of GSOs changed and became increasingly profit-motivated. Now it is not uncommon to see GSOs change the rules of their sports to become more attractive to the television audience, and to reschedule events for peak TV viewing. In 1998 during the volleyball world championship, the women's teams were obliged to 'wear tight-fitting outfits cut in an upward angle toward the top of the leg to give the sport a more sexy image' (McComb 2004). Despite safety concerns, the Formula 1 owner Bernie Ecclestone has been actively pushing for night races in Asia to cater to the European audience and broadcasters. In 2008 the first F1 Grand Prix night race was launched in Singapore. Walsh and Giulianotti (2002) argue that GSOs make two types of decisions: '(a) decisions in which financial considerations are taken into account, and (b), decisions in which financial decisions are totally determining'. It is now commonplace for GSOs to establish specialised marketing departments to deal with commercial issues, and to assume an active role in marketing and economic activities.

For most GSOs, international professional competitions such as world championships become their most important marketing platform, and from the 1960s onwards, sports like rowing (1962), swimming (1973), and athletics (1983) organised world championships with the assistance of broadcasting revenue and sponsorship. In turn, global broadcasting and marketing of these events have made many GSOs and their events globally recognised brands that multinational corporations compete to associate with.

Following FIFA and the IOC, more and more GSOs now take a central role in negotiating broadcasting contracts, and it has become commonplace for GSOs to set up global partnership schemes, particularly in the area of sponsorship. IAAF declared that: 'The Official Partners of the IAAF provide our sport with the means to develop and grow. They are an essential part of the world-wide family of athletics' (IAAF 2010).

With the enormous sums obtained through broadcasting rights, corporate sponsorship and other commercial activities, many GSOs have become exceedingly rich. Even the IOC, arguably the most powerful GSO in the world, had little income until broadcasting revenue started in the 1960s. Before that, 'rich men ran the IOC' and paid their own expenses (McComb 2004). The IOC earned US$3.5 billion overall from broadcasting, sponsorships, licensing and other commercial income between 1997 and 2000 (IOC 2001; cf. Forster 2004). FIFA's revenues have grown to over US$4 billion over the four-year interval between World Cups. As *The Economist* (2011) pointed out (under a photograph of a line of pigs all with their snouts in the trough):

> In the four years up to 2010, after its contribution to the costs of the World Cup in South Africa, FIFA made a profit of $631m and kept a handsome $707m for its own operating expenses, while dispensing $794m to its 208 grateful member football associations, many of them poor and dependent on FIFA's largesse.

For the International Rugby Board (IRB), its revenue from broadcasting of the World Cup increased from a mere £1 million in 1987 to £45 million in 1999, and over the same period, sponsorship income rose from £2 million to £17 million (Forster and Pope 2004).

GSOs' growing economic power and their new role of revenue generation and distribution has led to the argument that ends and means of the GSOs have become inverted. Sport is 'no longer their objective but a means to other more economically oriented organizational ends' (Forster and Pope 2004). As a result, their status of being non-profit-making is increasingly called into question. Questions have been raised over their capacity 'to act simultaneously as regulatory institutions and as commercial entities in the negotiation of sponsorship and broadcasting rights' (Lee 2005). This is parti-cularly controversial when there is a lack of transparency and accountability in the global governance of sports and sporting events and when 'representatives of governing hierarchies have frequently been accused of bribery and corruption' (Lee 2005). The Salt Lake City Olympics scandal involving bribery in the bidding process eventually led to the resignation of four IOC members and expulsion of another six. In late 2010, FIFA awarded Qatar the 2022 World Cup amid allegations that the decision was influenced by bribes. In 2011, Sepp Blatter was re-elected president of FIFA unopposed after his only rival, Qatar's Mohamed Bin Hammam, withdrew after allega-tions of bribery. How to achieve a compromise between the responsibility of non-profit governance as sports governing bodies and the newly assumed commercial role is going to be one of the most salient challenges that GSOs will continue to face in the future.

The economics of GSOs today

This raises the question of whether economic theory has anything to contribute to the understanding of the current situation of GSOs, as the Weisbrod non-profit model has little relevance for most GSOs in the current global commercial environ-ment. Weisbrod's (1998) more recent book, *To profit or not to profit: the commercial transformation of the nonprofit sector*, would seem from the title to offer a solution. Weisbrod (1998) argues that although the non-profits still have the provision of collective goods as their core mission, rises in their costs and/or inability to increase their revenues from donations and members' subscriptions, have led them to provide in addition private goods in competition with other non-profits and commercial providers. This can create a dilemma since often the non-profits may be receiving subsidies and tax advantages from government because of their role in providing collective goods, giving them an unfair advantage in the market for these private goods.

Although the title of this book seems appropriate, there is little in the approach taken in the book that can be applied to the economics of GSOs in the modern commercial environment. The reason is that Weisbrod is dealing with non-profits in the USA predominantly in the health, education and cultural sectors where these non-profits (e.g. health charities, non-profit hospitals and universities) are numerous and compete with each other and with other private providers. They are under the control of the government of the USA and are subject to regulation.

The big difference with GSOs is that they are international. The IOC and FIFA both have their headquarters in Switzerland, as do many other GSOs, where the secrecy of the banking system is a major advantage in keeping the financial operations non-transparent. The Swiss government does not directly regulate these GSOs, or at least has not done so up to now. The main distinction, however, between the situation analysed by Weisbrod (1998) for non-profits in the USA and the GSOs is that the GSOs have a monopoly position in their supply of major sports events. The commercial income of the IOC and FIFA has expanded massively over the last 30 years, but these GSOs are still mainly in the role of supplying the Olympics and the World Cup just as they were 30 years ago. The difference is that the demand for these events from host cities, broadcasters and sponsors has increased and since there is only one monopoly supplier and supply is fixed, this increase in demand has led to the huge rise in commercial income. The GSOs are in a unique market environment and Weisbrod's analysis simply is not appropriate.

There is a small literature, however, addressing the economics of the GSOs directly in the modern commercial environment. Forster and Pope (2004) attempted to look at several theoretical explanations of the behaviour of GSOs. They concluded:

> There is no single theoretical structure that is presently capable of providing even an adequate interpretation of the GSOs and their internal driving forces. … However, we outlined some areas where there is a an especial need for explanation to be strived for. One of these is the way their self-prescribed role in global society is either catered for or otherwise affects the internal workings of these organisations. Or, is it, as we venture to suggest little more than persiflage that obscures their real contribution to global culture in the form of sport. If so this makes the argument that ends and means of the GSOs have become inverted all the more important. Sport is no longer their objective but a means to other more economically oriented organisational ends.
>
> (Forster and Pope 2004: 114)

Forster and Pope argue that the objectives of GSOs have changed as a result of the commercialisation process. They put forward an ends-means inversion hypothesis:

> This states that non-profit organisations have a tendency for: (1) their original ends of objectives and (2) their financial means of achieving those ends to become inverted.
>
> (Forster and Pope 2004: 102)

The original objectives of GSOs, as we have seen, were to promote their sport and organise international competitions. Member organisations supported these objectives by providing financial support. Gradually GSOs obtained independent sources of finance mainly through their ownership of broadcasting and sponsorship rights to their global sports events and as a result became less dependent on these member associations. Instead of being dependent on their national associations, it became the reverse with the national associations becoming dependent on the GSOs.

> As this continued, the GSOs' relationship to sport was also changing. Sport was now required to contribute to the GSO. As a result, the member federations found themselves the servants of the GSOs. Finally the sport – via the global event controlled and owned by the GSO – became the means by which the GSO attained its financial goals and asserted its dominance.
>
> (Forster and Pope 2004: 102)

Unlike in Weisbrod's (1998) model, the GSOs do not engage in commercial activity to support their core mission. The commercial activity has been developed from that core mission but in the course of this development, the commercial activity itself has taken over as the end with the means being sport.

Case study of the IOC

Revival of the Modern Olympics

The revival of Modern Olympics is widely credited to Pierre de Coubertin, on whose initiative the International Athletic Congress of Paris was held in June 1894. The International Olympic Committee (IOC) was created on 23 June 1894, and the first Olympic Games of modern times were celebrated in Athens, Greece, in 1896 (Olympic Charter 2007).

The IOC claimed universal ideals and values ever since its inception. For de Coubertin and the other founding fathers of the IOC, the renewing of the ancient Olympic movement was more than sport, rather their main priority was 'the idea of peace among nations' (Müller 2006).

Eighty per cent of the honorary members of the IOC Founding Congress 1894 in Paris were members of national peace movements. Five of these later won Nobel Peace Prizes. De Coubertin was convinced that peace education could only be effective if theoretical learning was accompanied by personal experience. Olympic sport was the very means to achieve this aim. Sport in that sense should become an instrument to reform economy and politics and thus society as a whole: 'The Olympic Games will be a potent, if indirect factor in securing universal peace' (Müller 2006).

Today, the philosophy of promoting world peace through sport is still enshrined in the Olympic Charter: 'The goal of the Olympic Movement is to contribute to building a peaceful and better world by educating young people through sport practiced in accordance with Olympism and its values' (Olympic Charter 2007, Rule 1).

Unfortunately, the Olympic Games not only failed to prevent wars from happening, but had to be cancelled during both World Wars in the twentieth century.

Role and organisational structure of the IOC

From a legal standpoint, the IOC is an international non-governmental non-profit organisation based in Lausanne, Switzerland, of unlimited duration, in the form of an association with the status of a legal person, recognised by the Swiss Federal Council (ruling of 17 September 1981) (IOC 2010). The International Olympic Committee (IOC), created in 1894, is a non-governmental organisation with volunteer members who represent its work around the world.

According to its charter, the IOC governs the organisation, action and operation of the Olympic Movement and sets forth the conditions for the celebration of the Olympic Games. The Olympic symbol, flag, motto, anthem, identifications (including but not limited to 'Olympic Games' and 'Games of the Olympiad'), designations, emblems, flame and torches, shall be collectively or individually referred to as 'Olympic properties'. Essentially, 'all rights to any and all Olympic properties, as well as all rights to the use thereof, belong exclusively to the IOC, including but not limited to the use for any profit-making, commercial or advertising purposes' (Olympic Charter 2007).

The three pillars of the Olympic Movement are the International Olympic Committee (IOC), the International Sports Federations (IFs), and the National Olympic Committees (NOCs). Among them, the IOC is the supreme authority of the movement; IFs are international non-governmental organisations recognised by the International Olympic Committee (IOC) as administering one or more sports at world level. The IFs have the responsibility and duty to manage and monitor the everyday running of the world's various sports disciplines and the practical organisation of events during the Games. The NOCs are the organisations that develop, promote and protect the Olympic Movement in their respective countries, and they are also the only organisations that can select and designate the city which may apply to organise the Olympic Games in their respective countries.

The powers of the IOC are exercised by its organs, namely:

1   the Session,
2   the IOC Executive Board,
3   the President.

Members of the IOC represent and promote the interests of the IOC and of the Olympic Movement in their own countries. They are volunteers who represent the IOC and Olympic Movement in their country (they are not delegates of their country to the IOC). Members of the IOC will not accept from governments, organisations, or other parties, any mandate or instructions liable to interfere with the freedom of their action and vote.

The economic transformation of the Olympics and changing role of the IOC

The early modern Olympic Games were linked to World Expos, and the 1900 Paris Games and the 1904 St Louis Games had few spectators but 'were peripheral aspects of great trade shows' (Tomlinson 2005). Despite these humble beginnings, in just over a century, the modern Olympics have evolved into the world's most popular cultural event and a global spectacle. Throughout these years, the Olympics and its governing body, the IOC, have undergone enormous changes and transformations. Since the 1960s, US broadcasting networks have witnessed intense bidding wars for the Olympic broadcasting rights, leading to steady and spectacular growth in television rights revenue for the Olympic Games.

By the 1980s, with the assistance of global satellite television, the Olympic Games had already gained worldwide popularity and had become a global media event. Its commercial potential, however, still remained largely untapped. Samaranch's predecessors had made continuous efforts to resist commercialisation and professionalism. Also, the IOC was 'innocent and naïve in terms of the commercial exploitation of its product, which left the Olympics open to exploitation by bodies with a more basic commercial rationale' (Tomlinson 2005).

TABLE 3.2 USA Summer Olympic TV rights fees

Year	City, Network	Hours	Fee
1960	Rome (CBS)	20	$394k
1964	Tokyo (NBC)	14	$1.5m
1968	Mexico City (ABC)	43.75	$4.5m
1972	Munich (ABC)	62.75	$7.5m
1976	Montreal (ABC)	76.5	$25m
1980	Moscow (NBC)	150	$87m
1984	Los Angeles (ABC)	180	$225m
1988	Seoul (NBC)	179.5	$300m
1992	Barcelona (NBC)	161	$401m
1996	Atlanta (NBC)	171	$456m
2000	Sydney (NBC/cable)	442	$705m
2004	Athens (NBC/cable)	1210	$793m
2008	Beijing (NBC/cable)	2200	$894m
2012	London (NBC/cable)	3500	$1.181b

Source: ABC, NBC, CBS

TABLE 3.3 USA Winter Olympic TV rights fees

Year	City, Network	Hours	Fee
1960	Squaw Valley (CBS)	15	$50k
1964	Innsbruck (ABC)	17.25	$597k
1968	Grenoble (ABC)	27	$2.5m
1972	Sapporo (NBC)	37	$6.4m
1976	Innsbruck (ABC)	43.5	$10m
1980	Lake Placid (ABC)	53.25	$15.5m
1984	Sarajevo (ABC)	63	$91.5m
1988	Calgary (ABC)	94.5	$309m
1992	Albertville (CBS/Turner)	116	$243m
1994	Lillehammer (CBS)	119.5	$300m
1998	Nagano (CBS)	123 5/6	$375m
2002	Salt Lake City (NBC/cable)	376	$545m
2006	Turin (NBC/cable)	416	$613m
2010	Vancouver (NBC/cable)	835	$820m

Source: ABC, NBC, CBS

It is generally recognised that the early 1980s represented a watershed in Olympic history (Tomlinson 2005; McComb 2004; Whannel 2005). This was the period when the IOC, under Samaranch's presidency, took a series of important decisions that transformed the finances of the Games and moved them towards full commercialisation and professionalisation.

In 1981, not long after Juan Samaranch became president of the IOC, the international sports federations were given the right to determine which athletes could compete in the Olympics. As a result, the door was opened for nations to admit professional athletes.

In 1982, the IOC established the 'New Source of Financing Commission' to exploit all new sources of additional revenue (Preuss 2004). In 1983, the IOC voted to allow the Games to be opened up to corporate sponsorship.

The 1984 Olympics served as a milestone in commercialisation of the Games. With the growing scale of the Games and the rising cost of staging them, the Olympics were increasingly seen as a financial burden and political risk to the host city. This was especially the case after the 1976 Montreal Games left the city with a huge debt of billions of dollars. The following Moscow Games cost the Soviet government an unknown sum of money, and suffered a boycott from the West led by the United States. As a result, Los Angeles became the only city to bid for the 1984 Games after the withdrawal of its only competitor, Teheran. To avoid a similar prospect of financial disaster, the city of Los Angeles passed a resolution that no municipal funds could be spent on the 1984 Games. The Los Angeles Olympic Organizing Committee with Peter Ueberroth as the president had to rely solely on private funding.

Ueberroth personally negotiated the television contracts and pushed the total broadcasting rights fee to an unprecedented US$286 million (McComb 2004). By limiting the number of sponsorship categories and guaranteeing exclusive rights in each category, the total sponsorship and licensing revenue reached a record high of

US$126.7 million, compared to a mere US$7 million at the 1976 Games. Through this maximisation of commercial income, the Los Angeles Games did report an unprecedented surplus of US$223 million. The 1984 Games is described as the beginning of the most successful era of corporate sponsorship in Olympic history (Smart 2007). These are only the second ever modern Games to generate a profit, the first being the 1932 Los Angeles Games. As Tomlinson (2005) indicates:

> The central characteristic of the model was the commercialisation of the event, a ruthless commodification of the product, only possible in a wholesale aban-donment of the amateur principle and ethos underpinning earlier Games, alongside a recognition that just as the Games themselves were fully exploited for their commercial potential, athletes themselves could make the most of their individual market potential.
>
> (Tomlinson 2005)

The success of the 1984 Games greatly promoted the influence and popularity of the Olympics and stimulated a strong interest in cities to host the Games. Following the 1988 Olympics, the Games had moved from 'an era in which they were associated with political protests and boycotts, and economic problems, into an era in which they were perceived as part of economic success and building city image' (Whannel 2005). This has led to strong competition between cities in bidding for subsequent Games and a further rise in both broadcasting rights fees and corporate sponsorship.

By the 1980s, the escalation in rights payments came to the point that it was in danger of outstripping the level of advertising revenue generated during broadcasts. When ABC paid US$309 for the 1988 Winter Olympics to retain its 'Olympic Network' tag, it was widely recognised in the television industry, including ABC itself, that the payment was too high and could not be recouped in advertising revenue (Whannel 2005). Despite this danger, the enthusiasm for winning the Olympics among US networks has continued right into the twenty-first century (see Tables 3.2 and 3.3). In 2003, seven and nine years before the actual events were to take place and with the host cities still to be selected, NBC paid $820 million for the 2010 Winter Games and $1.181 billion for the 2012 Summer Olympics.

Since the 1980s, the world outside the USA has also started to witness dramatic growth in the broadcasting rights fees for the Olympics. By the 1996 Atlanta Games, the proportion of television rights fees provided by the rest of the world rose to 49 per cent, compared with only 15 per cent in 1980 for the Moscow Olympics, and this share has remained over 40 per cent ever since.

The total rights fees for the 2010–12 Olympics rose to a spectacular $2.001 billion, representing a 33 per cent boost from the $1.508 billion for the 2006–8 Games (Martzke 2003).

Sponsorship revenue also rose dramatically after 1984. As Tomlinson (2005) points out: 'It is illuminating that entrepreneurial operators from outside the IOC were the ones to see the potential of the commercialisation process'. It was Horst Dassler, Chief Executive of Adidas, who helped revolutionise Olympic finances. Dassler established International Sports Leisure Marketing (ISL) in 1982 to market the FIFA global sponsorship programme. In 1982–3, ISL and the IOC established a partnership aimed at the worldwide marketing of the Games, and launched the Olympic Programme (TOP) (now known as the Olympic Partners) since 1985. The programme offers official Olympic Worldwide partner status and exclusive global marketing rights to a few select corporations who pay huge sum for Olympic sponsorship (Smart 2007; Horne and Manzenreiter 2006; Tomlinson 2005). For example, the 11 partners for the TOP programmes for the 2005–8 period brought in US$866 million (Smart 2007).

In 1986, the IOC voted to change the schedule of the Olympics, to exploit better the commercial potential of the Games. Starting in 1988, the Summer Games and the Winter Games were scheduled to take place two years apart from each another, rather than in the same year.

One notable change since the 1980s is that the IOC has started to assume a central role over the key negotiations regarding television revenue and sponsorship (Whannel 2005). The IOC has negotiated the television rights alone since 1992 (Preuss 2004). In order to establish the TOP programme and market the Games to sponsors centrally, the IOC persuaded the National Olympic Committees to relinquish their own local rights in the key product areas (Whannel 2005).

On the one hand, this central role of the IOC has greatly improved its power in the negotiations and helped to foster long-term partnerships with broadcasting networks and corporations. On the other hand, the IOC has become increasingly involved in profit seeking and revenue generation activities. As a result, the IOC is now one of the most financially secure GSOs in the world but this has been achieved at the expense of substantial criticism that the original ideals of the Olympic Movement have been lost along the way as the quote below from MacAloon (2011) illustrates:

> My critical position ... is rooted in the distinction between the Olympic Movement and the Olympic Sports Industry (OSI). The latter can be thought of as Olympic sport without Olympism, or stated more precisely, the OSI, as an ideal type, reverses the means/ends relationship between sport and the intercultural, diplomatic and educational meanings characteristic of the Olympic Movement. For the OSI, Olympic symbols, values, social projects and histories are mere instrumentalities available for the expansion of Olympic-style competitions, for the 'growth of the brand' as many of its paid professionals like to put it ... my decades of Olympic research had led me to the conviction that the Olympic Movement was in ever-increasing danger of being swallowed up by the OSI.
>
> (MacAloon 2011)

4

GLOBAL SPORTS EVENTS

Introduction

What has given the major GSOs their economic power has been their exclusive ownership of major sports events. As some of these events have become global over the last three
to four decades, so the monopoly power of the GSOs has increased in particular in the
global broadcasting market and in the global sponsorship market for the rights to broadcast
and sponsor these events. The two most powerful GSOs, the IOC and FIFA, own the
two most popular sports events on the planet, the Olympics and the football World Cup,
and these two events will be the focus of this chapter. Not only do the majority of the
world's population watch these events live on television, but also major cities and countries all over the world compete intensely to host these events. Not all GSOs' own events
are as popular with both the viewing public and the hosting cities as those owned by the
IOC and FIFA. It is still the case, however, that for many GSOs, it is the ownership of
events that attracts global media coverage which determines their economic power.

In the last chapter, we looked at the supply side of the market for events, the role
of the GSOs that own them. In this chapter, we shall look at the demand side of the
event market. Why do major cities around the world compete so fiercely to host
global sports events? What are the benefits to them of hosting such events?

The economic benefits of hosting major sports events

The economic benefits of hosting major sports events have become an increasingly
controversial part of event literature. Many governments around the world have
adopted national sports policies that specify that hosting major sports events is a major
objective. A broad range of benefits has been suggested for both the country and the
host city from staging major sports events including: economic impact, urban regeneration legacy benefits, sport development benefits, tourism and image benefits, place
marketing benefits, and social and cultural benefits.

Over the past three decades, more and more cities throughout North America, Europe, Australia and elsewhere have joined the competition to host major sports events for a broad range of claimed benefits from immediate economic impact to long-term legacies such as image enhancement and sports infrastructure (Hall 2004; Gratton et al. 2005). The study of major sports events started to attract growing academic interest since the 1980s (Gratton et al. 2001; Horne and Manzenreiter 2006). While the economic impact of such events has been the main focus of this literature (Crompton 2001; Gratton et al. 2005), it is also the most controversial area that has been fiercely debated. For example, there was substantial debate over the size of the economic benefits of the Formula 1 Grand Prix held in Melbourne in 1996 (Hall 2006). Authors have often reached very different, if not opposite, conclusions about the economic benefits of the same events by using different methods and measurement. While one assessment of the 1996 Grand Prix indicated that it provided a gross economic benefit to the Victorian economy of Australian $95.6 million and created 2,270 full-time equivalent jobs, a different evaluation concluded that the claim of $95.6 million of extra expenditure was a misrepresentation of the size of the economic benefit and that the gross benefits were non-existent (Hall 2006).

Mules and Faulkner (1996) point out that even with such mega–events as Formula 1 Grand Prix races, it is not always an unequivocal economic benefit to the cities that host the event. They emphasise that, in general, staging major sports events often results in the city authorities losing money even though the city itself benefits greatly in terms of additional spending in the city. Thus the 1994 Brisbane World Masters Games cost the city $2.8 million to organise but generated a massive $50.6 million of additional economic activity in the State economy. Mules and Faulkner's basic point is that it normally requires the public sector to finance the staging of the event and incurring these losses in order to generate the benefits to the local economy. They argue that governments host such events and lose taxpayers' money in the process in order to generate spillover effects or externalities.

In addition to the study of the economic impact of major sports events, there is also growing literature on social and other benefits of major sports events (Hall 1992; Chalip et al. 2003; Chalip 2004; Chalip and Costa 2005; Smith 2002, 2005; Xing and Chalip 2006). Some argued that social benefits may be greater in the long term than the immediate economic impact generated by visitors' spending at these events (Crompton 2001; Liu and Gratton 2010).

It is not a straightforward job, however, to establish a profit and loss account for a specific event. Major sports events require investment in new sports facilities and often this is paid for in part by central government. Thus some of this investment expenditure represents a net addition to the local economy since the money comes in from outside. Also such facilities remain after the event has finished, acting as a platform for future activities that can generate additional tourist expenditure (Mules and Faulkner 1996).

The Commonwealth Games held in Manchester in 2002 involved an investment of £200 million in sporting venues in the city and a further £470-million investment in transport and other infrastructure. Most of the money for infrastructure investment came from central government in terms of urban regeneration funding and investment in sporting infrastructure was mainly from the National Lottery. Thus, most of the additional investment for the event was financed from outside Manchester and represented a net economic benefit to the city. This is by far the largest investment related to the hosting of a specific sports event ever to be undertaken in Britain prior to the investment for the London Olympics in 2012. It was also the first time in Britain that planning for the hosting of a major sports event was integrated within the strategic framework for the regeneration of the city, in particular East Manchester (Gratton and Preuss 2008).

Crompton (2001) identified four additional lines of argument that have been widely used to generate support for major investments of public funds in the construction of major sports facilities and events: increased community visibility; enhanced community image; stimulation of other development such as upgrading or initiation of businesses; and psychic income.

Sports events are increasingly seen as part of a broader tourism strategy aimed at raising the profile of a city and therefore success cannot be judged on a simple profit and loss basis. Often the attraction of events is linked to a re-imaging process, and in the case of many cities, is linked to strategies of urban regeneration and tourism development (Bianchini and Schwengel 1991; Bramwell 1995; Roche 1994). Major events, if successful, have the ability to project a new image and identity for a city. The hosting of major sports events is often justified by the host city in terms of long-term economic and social consequences, directly or indirectly resulting from the staging of the event (Mules and Faulkner 1996). These effects are primarily justified in economic terms, by estimating the additional expenditure generated in the local economy as the result of the event, in terms of the benefits injected from tourism related activity, and the subsequent re-imaging of the city following the success of the event (Roche 1992).

City image is generally referred to as the overall impression that a city creates in the minds of various target groups, including its functional and symbolic elements, and it encompasses the city's physical attributes, services, attraction, name, logo, reputation and the benefits that these provide to the target groups (Walmsley and Young 1998). A city's image can be enhanced or changed, and the deliberate use of various strategies to form, enhance, or change a city's image by city marketers is often called 'city branding' or 'city imaging'. The value of such image enhancement is that it can attract new tourists and/or new business and investment to the destination (Liu and Gratton 2010).

As an example, one of the aims of hosting the FIFA Football World Cup 2006 was to reposition the stereotype of Germans being 'conformist, time-dominated, serious' (Lewis 2006: 223). The organisers and government launched a hospitality concept including location-marketing for Germany, a cultural programme and a service and friendliness campaign. Another example is Qatar hosting the 2006 Asian Games in Doha. Ultimately, the country was trying to reposition its image and infrastructure to become the Arabic sport and entertainment centre. Mega sports events are often used as a catalyst to transform a location into a tourist destination. This corporate-centre strategy requires the building of convention centres, sports facilities, museums, shopping malls and entertainment and gambling complexes to reach economic growth by consumption-orientated economic development.

Cities staging major sports events have a unique opportunity to market themselves to the world. Increasing competition between broadcasters to secure broadcasting rights to major sports events has led to a massive escalation in fees for such rights, which in turn means broadcasters give blanket coverage at peak times for such events, enhancing the marketing benefits to the cities that stage them.

Such benefits might include a notional value of exposure achieved from media coverage and the associated place marketing effects related to hosting and broadcasting an event which might encourage visitors to return in future, or alternatively an investigation into any sports development impacts, which may encourage young people to get more involved in sport. Collectively, these additional benefits could be monitored using a more holistic approach to event evaluation.

Legacy

In the existing literature on social and long-term impact of sports events, the concept of legacy has been used with increasing frequency. The popularity of the word legacy is largely due to its association with the Olympic discourse, referring to the long-lasting impacts of Olympic movement and Olympic Games. In 2000, the Olympic Games Global Impact (OGGI) project was launched by the IOC to improve the evaluation of the overall impacts of the Olympic Games on the host city, its environment and its citizens, as well as to propose a consistent methodology to capture the overall effects of hosting the games (Gratton and Preuss 2008). The concept of 'legacy', together with the concept of 'sustainable sports development', has become an essential part of the IOC and the Organising Committee of the Olympic Games (OCOG) vocabulary (Girginov and Hills 2008).

Despite the lack of a clearly defined concept, more and more authors tend to agree that legacies of major sports events such as the Olympics could be positive or negative, tangible or intangible, intended or untended (Mangan 2008; Gratton and Preuss 2008; Masterman 2009), and authors have proposed different perspectives on possible event legacies.

There is a growing awareness that more research needs to be done to gain a comprehensive understanding of the impact of mega sporting events such as the Olympics. Roche (2006) stated that research of the Olympic impact needed support from relevant national and international social science research funding authorities, from the IOC and from Games event organising committees, and it is unfortunate that progress in achieving that 'does not seem to have been a feature of the Athens Olympic Games held in 2004, just as it wasn't a feature of Atlanta 1996 or Sydney 2000'. He must be disappointed again, as so far no result has been revealed from the 2008 Olympic Games Impact project, despite its launch at the beginning of the century.

The economic importance of the summer Olympic Games

Despite the huge sums of money invested in hosting the summer Olympics there has never been an economic impact study to assess the economic benefits of hosting the event. Kasimati (2003) summarised the potential long-term benefits to a city of hosting the summer Olympics: newly constructed event facilities and infrastructure, urban revival, enhanced international reputation, increased tourism, improved public welfare, additional employment and increased inward investment. In practice, however, there is also a possible downside to hosting the event including: high construction costs of sporting venues and related other investments, in particular in transport infrastructure, temporary congestion problems, displacement of other tourists due to the event, and underutilised elite sporting facilities after the event which are of little use to the local population.

Kasimati (2003) analysed all impact studies of the summer Olympics from 1984 to 2004 and found, in each case, that the studies were done prior to the Games, were not based on primary data, and were, in general, commissioned by proponents of the Games. He found that the economic impacts were likely to be inflated since the studies did not take into account supply side constraints such as investment crowding out, price increases due to resource scarcity, and the displacement of tourists who would have been to the host city had the Olympics not been held there.

Although no proper economic impact study using primary data has ever been carried out for the summer Olympics, Preuss (2004) has produced a comprehensive analysis of the economics of the summer Olympics for every summer Games from Munich 1972 using secondary data, and employing a novel data transformation methodology which allows comparisons across the different Olympics.

Despite collecting a massive amount of secondary data, Preuss's conclusion on the estimation of the true economic impact of the summer Olympics is the same as Kasimati's: 'The economic benefit of the Games ... is often overestimated in both publications and economic analyses produced by or for the OCOG [Organising Committee of the Olympic Games] ... multipliers tend to be too high and the number of tourists is estimated too optimistically.'

Preuss, however, does make some strong conclusions from his analysis. He shows, for instance, that every summer Olympics since 1972 made an operational surplus that the OCOG can spend to benefit both national and international sport. Stories relating to massive losses from hosting the Olympics have nothing to do with the Games' operational costs and revenues. Rather it is to do with the capital infrastructure investments made by host cities on venues, transport, accommodation and telecommunications. These are investments on capital infrastructure that have a life of 50 years or more and yet many commentators count the full capital cost against the two to three weeks of the Games themselves. Preuss points out that this is economic nonsense:

> it is impossible and even wrong to state the overall effect of different Olympics with a single surplus or deficit. The true outcome is measured in the infrastructural, social, political, ecological and sporting impacts a city and country receive from the Games.

Estimating the true economic impact of the summer Olympic Games properly therefore requires a huge research budget in addition to the other costs associated with the Games. Research needs to start several years before the Olympics and continue several years after they have finished. So far, nobody has been willing to fund such research. However, there is increasing research output relating to other major sporting events.

It is often argued, however, that such events generate a longer-term legacy of economic benefits. One example that is often quoted to support this argument is the case of the Barcelona Olympics in 1992.

Sanahuja (2002) provided evidence on the longer-term economic benefits of hosting the Olympics in Barcelona in 1992. The paper analysed the benefits to Barcelona in 2002, ten years after hosting the games. Table 4.1 shows almost a 100 per cent increase in hotel capacity, number of tourists, and number of overnight stays in 2001 compared to the pre-Games position in 1990. Average room occupancy had also increased from 71 per cent to 84 per cent. In addition, the average length of stay had increased from 2.84 days to 3.17 days. In 1990, the majority (51 per cent) of tourists to Barcelona were from the rest of Spain, with 32 per cent from the rest of Europe, and the remainder (17 per cent) from outside Europe. By 2001, the absolute number of Spanish tourists had actually risen by 150,000 but given the near doubling of the number of tourists overall, this higher total only accounted for 31 per cent of the total number of tourists. The proportion of tourists from the rest of Europe went up from 32 per cent to 40 per cent (representing an absolute increase of around 800,000) and from the rest of the world from 17 per cent to 29 per cent (representing an absolute increase of around 600,000).

Overall, infrastructure investment prior to the Games was $7.5 billion compared to a budget of around $1.5 billion for the Olympic Committee to stage the games. The Olympics in Barcelona were the most expensive ever staged prior to Beijing. However, Barcelona's use of the Games as a city marketing factor is generally regarded as a huge success.

TABLE 4.1 Legacy tourism benefits of Barcelona Olympics

	1990	2001
Hotel capacity (beds)	18,567	34,303
Number of tourists	1,732,902	3,378,636
Number overnights	3,795,522	7,969,496
Average room occupancy	71%	84%
Average stay (days)	2.84	3.17
Tourist by origin		
Spain	51.2%	31.3%
Europe	32%	39.5%
Others (USA, Japan, Latin America)	16.8%	29.2%

Source: Turisme de Barcelona (Barcelona's Tourist Board) and Sanahuja (2002)

TABLE 4.2 The best cities to locate a business today

	1990	2001	2002
London	1	1	1
Paris	2	2	2
Frankfurt	3	3	3
Brussels	4	4	4
Amsterdam	5	5	5
Barcelona	11	6	6
Madrid	17	8	7
Milan	9	11	8
Berlin	15	9	9
Zurich	7	7	10
Munich	12	10	11
Dublin	–	13	12

Source: Sanahuja (2002)

TABLE 4.3 Investment in general infrastructure: Beijing 2008

Investment composition	Amount in RMB (billion)	Amount in USD (billion)
Transportation	178.2	26.2
Energy infrastructure	68.5	10.0
Water resources	16.1	2.37
Urban environment	17.2	2.53
Total	280	41.1

This is evidenced by Barcelona's rise in Cushman and Wakefield's European Cities Monitor of the best European cities in which to locate a business: Barcelona was eleventh in 1990 and sixth in 2002 (see Table 4.2). Cushman and Wakefield has conducted this survey on Europe's major business cities each year since 1990. Senior executives from 500 European companies give their views on Europe's leading business cities.

By 2007 it had risen even higher to replace Brussels in fourth place. Barcelona is generally regarded as the most successful Olympics ever in terms of the long-term legacy effects on the city. It is impossible to evaluate fully the legacy benefits of the Beijing Olympics until 15 or 20 years have elapsed since the Games were hosted there. However, it is possible to point to a range of benefits that can already be seen to have resulted from the 2008 Beijing Olympics.

Case study: legacy of Beijing 2008

Gratton and Preuss (2008) identified six major legacy effects of major events: infrastructure; knowledge, skill development and education; image; emotions; networks; and culture. We consider these below in relation to the Beijing games and also add a seventh: the elite sports legacy.

Infrastructure

Infrastructure obviously means the sports infrastructure for competition and training, but also the general infrastructure of a city such as airports, roads, telecommunication, hotels, housing (athletes, media, and officials), entertainment facilities, parks, etc.

Beijing 2008 is often referred to as the most expensive Olympics ever staged with the often-cited figure of $40 billion of infrastructure investment. Both the actual figure and what it entails are worth further examination. China's National Audit Office released the final auditing result of the Beijing Games on 19 June 2009 (NAO report 2009), and from this auditing report in combination with figures released earlier by the Chinese authorities, a bigger picture of the cost of the event can be established. In general, there are three areas of cost often discussed with regard to the Olympics.

First is the cost of general infrastructure investment. According to the information released by a Beijing municipal government spokesperson at a press conference on 1 August before the Games, 'since 2001, the major infrastructure investment is a total of 280 billion RMB' (BOCOG 2008).

In a sense, to include the investment in general infrastructure in the cost of the Beijing Olympics is highly problematic, as on the one hand, 'all the projects are indeed in accordance with the Five-Year Plan for the city. These projects should be completed by 2010. That is to say because of the Games, these projects were done ahead of time' as the spokesman explained; on the other hand, as the economically fast-growing capital city of the most populous country in the world was aiming to become a modern metropolis, Beijing had already been investing and would continue to invest heavily on infrastructure construction anyway. It is expected that in the five years following the Beijing Olympics, the overall investment in infrastructure will exceed 350 billion RMB, even higher than the total investment in the seven years leading up to the Olympics (Chinanet 2008). In other words, the investment in general infrastructure before the Olympics is compatible with the urban development of the city. The Beijing Olympics obviously may have accelerated the infrastructure construction, but it would be inappropriate to treat the 280 billion RMB of general infrastructure as simply due to the Games.

Second, there is the sports infrastructure cost. As this part of the cost is directly attributed to the Games and is largely funded by public money, both the total cost and the post-Games use of the infrastructure is important as far as the event legacy is concerned. According to China's National Audit Office's report, total investment in the Beijing Olympic venues amounted to 19.49 billion RMB ($2.86 billion), covering 102 projects in Beijing and other co-host cities. The 102 projects consist of 36 competition venues and 66 training sites.

Third, there is the operating cost of the Games. The Beijing Organising Committee reported income of 20.5 billion RMB and expenses of 19.34 billion RMB for the 2008 Beijing Olympics with an operating profit of over 1 billion RMB ($146 million), but this profit did not take into account the 2.703 billion RMB of the special national grant coming from the lottery.

Following the Beijing Olympics, there has been substantial upgrading in the infrastructure in general, and in transport in particular (see Table 4.3 for the breakdown of investment in general infrastructure). The newly built airport terminal increased capacity by 24 million. Three new underground lines and one new express link from the airport to the city were built. 'Beijing subway extended from 42 kilometres to 200 kilometres, ... Beijing leads the whole country in terms of the cheap fares of the subway and public transportation' (BOCOG 2008). In 2006, 90 per cent of the wastewater in Beijing's eight districts was treated. In addition, 96.5 per cent of the domestic waste produced was treated and disposed of properly. Also in 2006, the city saw 241 days where the air quality index reached Grade 2 or better – an increase of 56 days over 2001. And the city's green coverage reached 42.5 per cent in 2006, with 12 square miles of green land per person (BOCOG 2007).

With regard to sports infrastructure, it does seem that both the cost of the venue and the post-event use of the venues have been taken into consideration in the venue planing as

> Beijing has made some big adjustments for the stadiums' construction scale, allocation and investment. The number of stadiums needed for the Games in Beijing was reduced from 32 to 31, of which, the newly constructed venues were cut from 19 to 12, venues to be renovated and expanded rose from five to 11, and eight temporary venues were added from zero.
>
> (Beijing Review 2008)

An example of the effort to control the venue budget is the changes made to the construction of the iconic Bird's Nest for the opening ceremony. The design team was asked to examine ways of reducing project costs, and as a result, the retractable roof was removed, leaving in its place a larger, permanent opening (Brown 2008).

In terms of post-event use, two factors were considered in the site selection. First was the amalgamation of Olympic venues with university venues construction to ensure the post-event use. Thus four out of the twelve newly built venues are located on campus of several major universities. The second is the density of population and current demand. For instance, the Wukesong Stadium is located in the west of Beijing where there was a lack of major sports facilities, and this stadium which is constructed according to NBA Standard will also be used as a standing venue by NBA China games.

The future of the two most high-profile venues, the Bird's Nest and the Water Cube, seem promising at the moment. Both venues have become Beijing's new landmarks and thus new tourist attractions. According to figures released by the capital's municipal tourism bureau, the Olympic Common Domain, where the Bird's Nest, the Water Cube and the National Indoor Stadium are located, has eclipsed Beijing's traditional attractions as tourists' first choice in the first Golden-week holiday in October after the Olympic Games (China Daily 2009).

According to the Citic Group, the management company of the Bird's Nest, in addition to tourism development, 'it will in three to five years build the National

Stadium into an entertainment and shopping centre, while seeking to hold more sports games and cultural performances' (People's Daily online 2009).

While the post-use of many of the venues seemed guaranteed, critiques also raised other problems. One of them was whether these sports infrastructures would serve only the rich and tend to discriminate against disadvantaged people. For instance, the ticket prices of 50 RMB and 30 RMB respectively for touring the Bird's Nest and the Water Cube are considered too high by many, and a survey conducted by *China Youth Daily* showed that 89.6 per cent of respondents called for public opening with discounted prices (China Youth Daily 2008).

Knowledge, skill-development and education

The host population gains knowledge and skills from staging a mega sports event. Employees and volunteers develop skills and knowledge in event organisation, human resource management, security, hospitality, service and so on.

What is noteworthy is the unprecedented scale of volunteers involved in the Beijing Games. According to Liu Jian, Director of the Volunteer Department of BOCOG, 1.7 million people served as volunteers in Beijing and the co-host cities, the highest in both Chinese and Olympic history for a single event, including 100,000 Games volunteers (30,000 of these being Paralympics volunteers) providing direct services at the official venues, 400,000 city volunteers providing visitor information, translation assistance, and so on, through designated volunteer posts, and one million 'society volunteers' engaging in routine services, plus 200,000 cheerleading volunteers (People's Daily 2008).

It is reported that the Games volunteers alone attracted over 1 million applications (Xinjing Daily 2008). The volunteers had to undergo systematic and intensive training to perform their jobs. For instance, the Games volunteers had to be trained in following areas:

> General training: basic Olympic knowledge, brief introduction to the Beijing Olympic and Paralympic Games, Chinese history and traditional culture, history and cultural life in Beijing, knowledge and skills necessary to serve the disabled, etiquette norm, medical knowledge and first-aid skills, etc.
>
> Professional training: professional knowledge and skills required in voluntary services.
>
> Venue training: venue functions, knowledge concerning the sports held in the venue, internal facilities, organisational structure, rules and regulations, etc.
>
> Job training: job responsibilities, specific works, business procedures, and operating norms, etc.
>
> (BOCOG 2006)

Many employers seemed to value highly people's work experience with Beijing Olympics when recruiting. A job fair specifically aimed at former BOCOG members took place two month after the Games and offered 1,753 posts to only some 1,500 applicants with supply exceeding demand for the first time in the Beijing job fair history (Jinghua Shibao 2008), which was even more striking given that thousands of people were still losing jobs because of the global economic crisis.

There was a particular step forward in Beijing in relation to knowledge of environmental policy. Half of the cars in Beijing were kept off the roads from mid-July to late September and there then followed a trial period when car owners could not use their car for one day a week. Dong and Mangan (2008) indicate the extent of attention to the environment:

> Beijing set a demanding target: by 2008, the days of air quality were to reach second or above grades for 75–80 per cent of the whole year. Accordingly a series of measures, including adjusting the industrial economic structure, controlling industrial pollution, suspending or closing seriously contaminated plants, removing the most pollutant plants from within the four ring-road systems, intensifying recycling, have been taken. In addition, the emission of waste gases has been reduced and environmental friendly methods adopted in several renovation projects, while about 200 factories threatening potentially empoisoning pollution were moved out of the city completely between 2002 and 2005.
>
> (Dong and Mangan 2008)

Dong and Mangan (2008) also point to the training initiatives carried out by BOCOG. A Coordination Committee for Competence was set up by BOCOG in 2005. This committee trained officials, sports managers, coaches and referees. Training was also provided for the media, security staff, and hosts and hostesses. BOCOG also selected people for special study abroad such as competition administrators who were attached to the Athens Organising Committee for six months.

In education, once the bid had been won, China instituted the Olympic Education Project involving 400 million students from 400,000 schools across the country, the biggest Olympic education initiative in history.

The Beijing Olympics also pushed English language study to a new height. As a newspaper observed:

> On July 13, tens of millions of Chinese viewers were surprised to see 69-year-old Vice-Premier Li Lanqing, and Liu Qi, mayor of Beijing, speaking in fluent English to the crucial IOC meeting in Moscow, which was broadcast live on China's national TV. The 58-year-old Beijing mayor later told reporters he practiced the presentation almost every day for two weeks.
>
> (People's Daily Online2001)

The authorities initiated various campaigns and schemes to improve the English skills of police, drivers, waitresses, volunteers and so on, and people were also highly motivated to learn English believing it would help them capitalise better on the opportunities brought by the Olympics.

Another important legacy was the improved good habits in public as a result of series of campaigns to promote good citizenship to present the best image to the world. A number of campaigns were launched in Beijing before the Games to improve people's manners and tackle bad habits such as spitting, queue jumping, littering. The Games also left long-lasting impacts in terms of growing awareness of environment protection, intellectual property rights and consideration of disabled people.

Image

Mega sports events have tremendous symbolic significance and form, and contribute to repositioning or solidifying the image of a city, region, and country. Usually events create a positive imagery and the city and politicians can 'bask in [its] reflected glory' (Snyder *et al.* 1986). On the other hand, the worldwide exposure of the event, the host city and its culture depends on the media representatives and cannot be entirely controlled by the organisers (Preuss and Messing 2002).

There is little doubt that the Beijing Olympics had a huge beneficial effect on China's image in the rest of the world. The opening ceremony stunned the world in its ambition and spectacle. Nothing like it had ever been seen before. The Bird's Nest stadium and the Water Cube also set new standards for international sporting venues and provided wonderful images seen by the entire world. Despite the opening up of China in recent decades, it was still a country that many people were not familiar with. The Olympics have changed that since two-thirds of the world's population saw Beijing and China every day for the best part of three weeks in August 2008.

According to the market research firm Nielsen, the Beijing Olympics attracted a record number of TV viewers both at home and abroad. It is said that about 94 per cent of the Chinese audience watched the Games, and in total they attracted about 4.7 billion TV viewers worldwide, surpassing the 3.9 billion who watched the 2004 Athens Games and the 3.6 billion viewers of the 2000 Sydney Games. Nielsen estimated that the dazzling opening ceremony alone on 8 August, led by film director Zhang Yimou, attracted almost one-third of the world's population, or about 2 billion TV viewers (China Daily 2008 September).

In addition to the massive TV exposure, Beijing Olympics was also covered by new media including the internet and mobile telephone media globally, for the first time in history. Nearly 6 million people visited the official website of the IOC, twice as many as during the Athens Games. Meanwhile, 28,000 journalists from across the world came to Beijing to cover the event (Xinhuanet 2008).

There will be both positive and negative coverage of the host city and host country. China, however, was determined to show the world her best face with modernity, friendliness, openness and efficiency and took enormous trouble and cost to achieve that end. The most controversial questions raised by the Western media for the Beijing Olympics were pollution, worries over security and human-rights issues. However, human rights issues have been the subject of a long term debate between the West and China and security turned out to be well under control.

Consequently, negative Western media coverage actually focused on the air quality in Beijing just days before the opening of the Games.

Beijing's huge investment in improvement of the environment in the run up to the Games and various measures taken such as traffic control, resulted in an improvement of the air quality, and 'worries over pollution and its impact on athletes seemed to fade away' (CNN 25 August 2008). In fact, when the Games concluded and Jacques Rogge, the IOC President, described them as 'truly exceptional', it was widely hailed by most major Western media as spectacular and grand (CNN 25 August 2008, Reuters 25 August 2008).

Emotion

Mega events generate pride for the population of the host city and country. In China, the Olympics were deliberately used to increase the confidence and self-esteem of the Chinese people. Part of this was related to the staging of the Games: the pride that comes from the association of this global event with one's own country. This was reinforced by the demonstration of Chinese culture at the opening ceremony. The euphoria generated in China by their topping the medal table added further to China's sense of national pride, self-esteem and confidence.

In a country like China that has suffered humiliation in its recent history, the generation of such national pride and self-esteem is particularly important. This was reflected in volunteer applications to for the Games where there were nearly 1 million applications for the 100,000 volunteer posts. A social survey in Beijing identified that 95 per cent of people in Beijing were willing to offer their services to the Games.

Ironically, the marginal loss of the 2000 Olympic bid to Sydney may have served to enhance the national pride of average citizens and their support for the 2008 Beijing Olympics. Compared to the massive domestic campaign to promote the 2000 Games bid, the authorities deliberately gave the 2008 bid a low profile at home to lower people's expectations, but a poll showed 94.4 per cent of Beijing citizens supported the bid, far exceeding the popular support of Beijing's rival (Guo Tingting 2001). The spontaneous celebration of the successful bid by the citizens shocked Western media, as illustrated by the BBC correspondent Matt Frei (2001): 'Genuine spontaneity in China is a rare thing. It can also be scary. … Tens of thousands of citizens, young and old, crying hysterically that China was finally going to … well … host a sports event. This was genuine Olympic fever.'

Networks

Major sports events require close cooperation between the international sports federation, the national sports federation, the local organising committee, politicians, the media, and a multitude of other organisations. The networks created through these interactions can lead to a lasting legacy from the event.

Owing to the massive scale and multi-year preparation and organisation needed, the Beijing Olympics greatly promoted international exchange in politics, culture, economics and sport and helped to build networks and links between China and the world. It was reported that over 550 Chinese schools conducted sport and educational exchanges with international counterparts (Xinhuanet 2008). The opening ceremony alone saw over 80 heads of state, leading government officials and royalty from more than 50 countries. The organisation of the Games will also strengthen China's ties with various international sports organisations especially the 28 international governing bodies of Olympic sports and help to secure China's future bids for major sporting events.

What is also noteworthy is the extensive international cooperation conducted in the run up to the Games. For instance, the EU–China Co-operation for Strategic Planning of Beijing Digital Olympics Programme (DOP) was launched for the successful organisation of the 2008 Beijing Olympics as well as long-term cooperation between the EU and China in the information society technology field. This programme, including such activities as establishing the EU–China Olympic Cities Forum to strengthen exchange of experience and knowledge related to development of the DOP, 'is believed to have provided a sound basis for a long-term and strong co-operation between the European and Chinese information society technology communities' (IST World).

Culture

Gratton and Preuss (2008) indicated how major events can leave a cultural legacy:

> Mega sport events produce cultural ideas, cultural identity and cultural products. Opening ceremonies especially include a cultural-artistic aspect which is a condensed display of the host country's culture. A positive cultural image, increased awareness, new infrastructure and additional tourist products, combined with the soft factor of better service quality have a great potential to increase tourism in the long-term.
>
> (Gratton and Preuss 2008)

Barcelona for instance used the Olympics to transform its infrastructure to become a 'cultural city' (Garcia 1993).

The Beijing Games was a celebration of both Olympic culture and Chinese traditional culture. The Olympic education project alone involved 400 million students from 400,000 schools across the country. From 2003 to 2008, the Ministry of Culture, the State Administration of Radio Film and Television, the State Physical Culture Administration, the Beijing government and the BOCOG jointly held the 2008 Olympic Cultural Festival on an annual basis. The final-year festival lasted nearly three months throughout the Olympic and Paralympic Games of 2008, featuring a series of important cultural activities including both China's national and world-class artistic performances. It was reported that nearly 20,000 artists from more than 80 countries participated in the performances with nearly 200 performances at 88 events as well as 600 performances in 254 events in Mainland China, Hong Kong, Macau and Chinese Taipei (BOCOG 2008 July).

The Beijing Olympics also helped the world understand Chinese culture better and attracted a growing number of people from overseas to learn the Chinese language, martial arts, and so on. In order to promote Chinese culture to readers at home and abroad, Chinese Cultural Reading, consisting of four parts and 37 chapters, was published in Chinese, English, French, German, Russian, Korean, and Spanish before the opening ceremony of the Beijing Olympic Games. Co-authored by Ye Lang and Zhu Liangzhi, professors in the Philosophy Department at Beijing University, it was meant to combine China's deep cultural mindset with its emotional contents (People's Daily Online 2008). It is estimated that there were 40 million non-Chinese learning the language worldwide in 2008 and the figure was growing by at least 10 million a year and was expected to reach 100 million by 2010 (Li 2008).

Elite sport legacy

The Beijing Olympics also produced an elite sport legacy. This could be part of the emotional legacy but we have chosen to treat it separately here because of its special significance to China. Xu (2008) indicated just how much sporting success meant to China:

> Since the 1980s the idea that winning is everything has entered the mindset of many Chinese, and the government has mobilised the nation's resources to achieve victories through administrative, legal, and political means … For the Chinese government, China's status and relative strength among nations became measured by the number of gold medals won at the Olympics.
>
> (Xu 2008: 215–16)

Shibli and Bingham (2008) showed that up to 2008 China had been very successful in improving its medal performance at the summer Olympic Games after it re-entered the competition in 1984, its first Olympics since the 1952 Helsinki Games. Figure 4.1 shows how China narrowed the gap between its own performance and that of the top performing nation in the summer Olympics between 1984 and 2004.

The figure included performance at the 2008 Olympics where China topped the medal table with 51 gold medals, 15 more than the next best nation, the United States. The United States did have 10 more medals than China when all medals are taken into account but as the quote from Xu above shows, it was gold medals that counted for China and topping the medals table was the objective which was achieved.

The last five hosts of the Olympic Games have performed better as hosts than they did in the preceding Olympics. Former host nations tend to experience a decline in their performance in the Olympics immediately after acting as hosts. However, this decline is to a higher level than pre-hosting performance which suggests that the Olympic Games can be a catalyst to bring about a sustainable step change in a nation's sporting competitiveness (Shibli 2008).

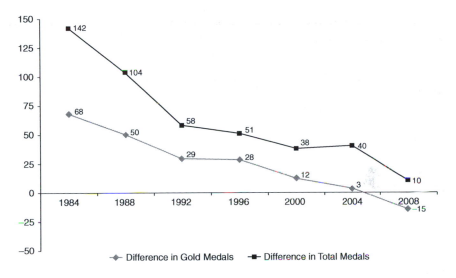

FIGURE 4.1 How China narrowed the gap between itself and the top-ranked nation
Source: Shibli and Bingham (2008)

Nations perform better as host than they do in the Olympics prior to hosting the Olympic Games. For elite sport, the legacy of being host is increased competitiveness in a greater number of sports at a higher level of success than prior to being host. Ten of the last 12 host nations have achieved their highest market share since 1948 in their host Games.

The most likely explanations for positive home advantage effects in the Olympic Games include: the right to contest more events; increased investment in elite sport; familiarity with venues and facilities; crowd impacts on home athletes; crowd impacts on officials in subjectively judged events; and, travel and disorientation impacts on rivals. The patterns in the data revealed by this research suggest that hosting the Olympic Games can provide a measurable longer-term elite sport development effect for host nations. This type of information is likely to increase further the demand for prospective nations to bid to host the Games in the future (Shibli 2008).

Figure 4.2 shows that China achieved the largest increase in market share of medals of any of the five immediate hosts of the Olympics prior to them: Greece, Australia, USA, Spain and Korea.

Figure 4.3 shows that China also won medals in 26 of the 41 Olympic sports, more than any of the previous five hosts of the Olympics. The Beijing Olympics hosted 28 sports but some of these were divided into several disciplines. For instance the sport of aquatics has four disciplines: swimming, diving, water polo and synchronised swimming. The steepness of the line between 2004 and 2008 in Figure 4.3 indicates a greater increase in breadth of performance for China than for any of the previous five hosting nations.

This success has not only contributed to the image and emotional legacies discussed above, it has also made China one of the major players on the world's sporting stage for the first time. At this point in time, China is the strongest Olympic nation in the

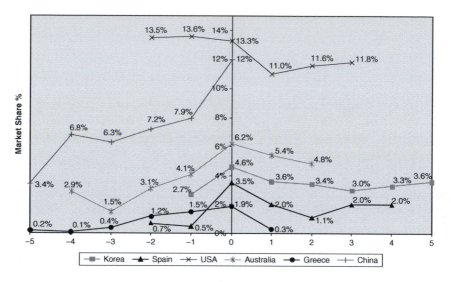

FIGURE 4.2 China's overall performance compared with the five previous hosts of the Summer
      Olympic Games
Source: Shibli and Bingham (2008)

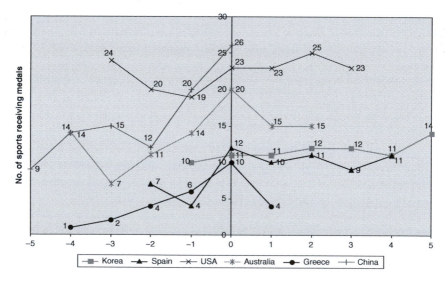

FIGURE 4.3 Breadth of medal-winning performance: number of sports in which medals were won
Source: Shibli and Bingham (2008)

world. Many commentators argued before the Beijing Games that if China topped
the medals table, the country would switch its emphasis from elite sport to grassroots
sport. However, once a country has achieved success like China, it is very difficult to
not attempt to build on this achievement. The likelihood is that China will attempt
to repeat that success in London and subsequent Olympics.

Conclusions

The literature on the economics of hosting major sports events has concentrated on whether or not these events generate significant economic impact for the host city and country. On the evidence collected at the Sydney, Athens and Beijing Olympics it seems the additional economic impact is very limited. In all three cases, the additional tourism generated by the Games was matched by a decline in the tourism that these cities generated on a regular basis. The non–sports tourists seem to avoid going to the cities while the Games are taking place, not least because hotel prices are at a premium for these weeks. The World Cup, on the other hand, does seem to make a greater economic impact. Ahlert and Preuss (2010) estimated that that German GDP increased by €3.2 billion during the 2006 World Cup. What we have seen in this chapter, however, is that the benefits of hosting major sports events are not only economic, but are also quite wide ranging. Whether the value of these benefits justifies the large investment required to host the Olympic Games is not clear. However, we have seen that most of the investment is on general infrastructure such as airports, rail and road transport infrastructure. Beijing needed a new airport, a new link form the city to the airport, and an expanded metro system. Hosting the Olympic Games simply brought this investment forward. The investment made by Barcelona in 1992 now supports a tourism market that has doubled since then. It will always be difficult to answer the question of whether the benefits outweigh the cost. The simple fact, though, is that there is huge competition between cities and countries to host these major events and that is why the GSOs that own these events continue to generate more and more revenue from selling them.

5

GLOBAL SPORT CORPORATIONS

Introduction

We saw in Chapter 3 that some GSOs had moved on from their original non-profit status to something similar to for-profit organisations maximising revenue from the sale of broadcasting rights and sponsorship for their major sports events. There are another set of organisations that also aim to maximise profit through their activities in the global sport market, transnational sports corporations. The literature on the economics of transnational corporations first began to develop in the 1980s (Dunning 1988). Virtually all the literature in the area of transnational corporations and global markets has ignored sport. Part of the reason for this is that sport is predominantly a service industry and the main focus of the literature has been on manufacturing industry. Segal-Horn (1989) has analysed the globalisation of service corporations but where services have been considered, emphasis has been placed on those services that are directly linked to manufacturing such as financial services and advertising. Also, sport is rarely treated as an industry in its own right by economists and therefore is never singled out for special analysis.

This chapter attempts to fill the gap and considers how to approach the study of transnational corporations in the sport industry. The first section of the chapter deals with conventional approaches to the study of transnational corporations. The second section identifies specific issues relevant to the operation of firms in sport and discusses theoretical issues in the study of transnational corporations in sport. The main question addressed is whether there are special factors present in the sport market that have a particular influence on the growth of global sport corporations. The theory is illustrated with several examples from the global sport market. The third section of the chapter goes into more detail using three specific case studies of transnational corporations in the sport industry.

Transnational corporations in a global competitive environment

The development of transnational corporations and the emergence of the concept of a global economic system is a relatively recent phenomenon. The first transnational corporations emerged in the primary sector, most notably in the oil industry, but the major development of transnational corporations in the manufacturing sector began in the 1950s with major investments in production capacity in Europe by US firms. In the 1960s and 1970s, European firms followed a similar transnational strategy with major investments in the USA. Japanese firms set up production facilities in Europe and the USA in the 1970s and 1980s and the most recent development is transnational firms emerging from the newly industrialising countries (NICs), most notably China, Korea and Singapore.

The motivation for large firms to move out of their own home markets and set up production facilities in foreign countries has varied over different stages of the development of the global economic system. The oil companies became transnational through the search for new sources of supply of the primary resource, oil. Initially, American and European manufacturing firms expanded abroad in search of new markets in pursuit of the firm's growth objective. In the 1970s and 1980s, these same firms were switching production from established areas and into cheaper production countries, most notably in the Far East. At the same time, Japanese firms and firms from the NICs were setting up production facilities in Europe and the USA, in order to overcome protectionist measures in those areas, which were restricting access to these lucrative markets.

The economic motivations for the development of TNCs and global orientation are well documented. The growth of TNCs involves a process of both corporate and territorial concentration. Corporate concentration refers to the tendency of a small number of very large firms to control a large percentage of output. Wallace (1990) summarises the economic forces leading to corporate concentration:

> This corporate concentration of production reflects a number of underlying pressures within a capitalist economy. One is that although the pursuit of profits and the pursuit of growth are not identical goals, they are in many respects interrelated. Economies of scale permit larger producers to undercut smaller producers and thereby increase their market share, and this process in itself gives the larger producer more power and flexibility in dealing with consumers. In sectors requiring very large capital investment per unit of output, such as the basic resource processing industries (metal refining, petrochemicals, and pulp and paper), there are often added technological arguments for large scale production. Economies of scope can be achieved by large multiproduct or multifunction firms which benefit from integrating a wide range of activities internally and reducing their transaction costs. As a firm's competitiveness becomes increasingly dependent on technological sophistication, requiring substantial investment in research and development (R&D) over a sustained period, there are further advantages which accrue to large producers who can

recoup these outlays from high volume sales. In many consumer goods sectors characterised by 'mature' products, such as detergents, the volume of sales which a particular firm can achieve depends on heavy advertising expenditures to maintain its 'brand image', which again favours large established producers. One or more of these characteristics can represent a barrier to entry which makes it increasingly difficult, if not impossible, for new firms to enter a given industry which has become dominated by a few large firms.

(Wallace 1990)

These economic forces leading to the growth of corporate concentration inevitably lead to some of the strongest firms expanding outside the original sector of activity (diversification) and/or outside of the original geographical market area (transnationalisation). Dunning (1988) refers to the advantages of large firms discussed above as 'ownership' advantages of the firm. The characteristics of the firm's home market and geographical position are referred to as 'locational advantages'. In a situation where ownership advantages are strong and location advantages weak, growth of the firm leads to expansion into foreign markets through direct foreign investment.

Much of this conventional discussion over the reasons for the growth of transnational corporations has focussed on firms in the manufacturing industry, or alternatively on firms operating in the primary sector (agriculture, minerals and other natural resources). Service industries have received little attention in the literature on TNCs largely because they have been perceived as fragmented industries characterised by low entry barriers and diseconomies of scale. However, Segal–Horn (1989) argues that this is an outdated view of service firms:

The sources of competitive advantage in service industries have shifted as a result of recent environmental, structural, market, and technological changes. This has provided a major shift in the potential for globalisation as a competitive strategy available to service industries. There exists now some evidence that, as already occurred in sizeable segments of manufacturing industry, those companies with clear strategic intent to leverage existing competitive advantage in support of long-term global brand dominance, can establish identifiable worldwide market presence.

(Segal-Horn 1989)

The next section concentrates on the forces operating on sports firms that are leading to a greater degree of internationalisation in the provision of sport.

Growth, concentration and internationalisation of sport corporations

As indicated earlier the development of transnational corporations is fuelled by the growth objective of firms. The argument presented in this section is that pursuit of this growth objective by sport corporations can lead to a variety of patterns of development in which internationalisation is increasingly involved. The analysis below is based to a large extent on the work of Penrose (1959).

Penrose developed a theory of the growth of firms. She was concerned neither with the internationalisation of firms nor with the sport industry but rather with growth and diversification of firms within their home markets. Gratton and Taylor (1987) applied her approach to leisure firms and in this chapter an attempt is made to extend it to the internationalisation of sport corporations.

Penrose adopted an unusual approach for an economist. She did not look at the firm as a theoretical concept with the cost curves and demand curves that appear in standard economics texts. Rather, she viewed the firm as a social and administrative organisation where people are particularly important for success or failure. The most important part of the organisation is the management team, which not only provides the motivation for growth and development, but is also likely to be the major constraint in the firm's rate of progress.

The basic motivation of management is the desire to increase total long-run profits. Since profits increase when investment yields a positive net return, then firms will expand 'as fast as they can take advantage of opportunities for expansion that they consider profitable'. The management must plan and organise the growth process. They must decide the speed of expansion, the route to growth, and then harness the firm's resources and administer the growth programme.

The initial phase of expansion will be determined by the firm's 'inherited resources', that is the productive services it already possesses. A quote from Penrose illustrates the growth process:

> There is no doubt that the growth of demand for a firm's existing products, as expressed through price changes and other sorts of market information, is a powerful influence on the direction of productive activity and on the expansion of firms. The possibility of expanding such demand by advertising and other sales efforts, and the effect of such efforts on the productive opportunity of the firm are not to be underestimated. Other things being equal, it is usually cheaper and less risky to expand the production of existing products than to enter new fields. When, therefore, the market demand for existing products is growing and entrepreneurs expect continued growth, 'demand' will appear as the most important influence on expansion and current investment plans may be closely tied to entrepreneurial estimates of the prospects for increasing sales in existing product lines. In an expanding economy, therefore, a large proportion of existing firms may be closely related to increased demand for their original types of product in much the same market area … demand for a firm's existing products will, therefore, have an important influence on the rate of growth of firms.
>
> (Penrose 1959)

In such an expanding market, the older established firms will have an advantage over newer firms and they will tend to grow faster. Those with the most alert and efficient management teams will grow fastest and we will therefore start to see concentration in the industry increasing. As the larger firms grow, they obtain further advantages from size, which gives them a further competitive edge over smaller firms, thus feeding the cycle of increasing concentration. Penrose argues that such a process cannot continue indefinitely. Even if demand continues to expand at the same rate, as the larger firms increase market share, their growth will be greater than the growth of demand. In order to continue to maintain such a growth rate, either industry demand will have to expand faster or the firm will have to expand its market share at the same rate. Since market share has a theoretical maximum of 100 per cent, and a realistic (or legally binding) maximum much less than this, then eventually it will become impossible to maintain the firm's growth rate without continual increases in the rate of growth of industry demand.

Thus, Penrose argues that demand acts as a constraint on a firm's growth even in industries where demand is expanding and this constraint leads the firm to expand outside its original market area. The question is what markets the firm will expand into.

The standard answer is that the company will continue to draw on its own expertise and knowledge. For a manufacturing firm, this will be knowledge of production technology. The obvious direction in which the firm will diversify is towards products that have a similar technological base, and there are many examples of such diversification in manufacturing industries. However, sport is primarily, though by no means totally, a service industry. Service industries do not have the technological production base to provide the platform for diversification. Management expertise and know-how in service industries is essentially marketing expertise. The nature of the demand for sport would suggest that the obvious area for the sport corporation to expand to is other international markets as the three case studies below illustrate.

Case studies in transnational sport corporations

Nike

Nike is a classic case-study of how the sport market has been affected by globalisation. Nike dominates the world sports shoe industry, an industry that has shown phenomenal growth over the last 20 years. Nike accounts for nearly a third of the total sales of sports shoes worldwide.

Nike started out as a company called Blue Ribbon Sports, based in Oregon, USA, and distributing running shoes produced by a Japanese company, Onitsuka Sports. By the early 1970s the company had severed ties with Onitsuka and was designing, marketing and distributing its own running shoes. In 1978 Blue Ribbon Sports changed its name to Nike. This company very quickly established itself in the lead in one of the fastest growing leisure markets in the world. Although Nike produces other sportswear, sports shoes are its main area of activity and 75 per cent of the company's turnover comes from shoes.

There is some literature relating to the global production, distribution, and marketing approach of Nike (Clifford 1992; Willigan 1992). What is perhaps surprising is that Nike is not a manufacturing company at all. All manufacturing is done by contractors, 99 per cent of them in Asia. Clifford (1992) described how Nike kept the cost of production down by constantly seeking out lowest-cost producers in the late 1980s and early 1990s:

> The company is forever on the lookout for cheap production sites. If costs in a particular country or factory move too far out of line, productivity will have to rise to compensate, or Nike will take its business elsewhere. The firm uses about 40 factories; 20 have closed in the past five years or so and another 35 have opened.
>
> (Clifford 1992: 59)

This tremendous dynamism and flexibility in the organisation of production is illustrated by Nike's response to soaring labour costs in South Korea in the late 1980s. In 1988, 68 per cent of Nike's shoes were produced in South Korea. By 1992, this percentage had fallen to 42 per cent (Clifford 1992). Over this period, Nike switched an increasing proportion of production to contractors in the cheaper labour cost countries of China, Indonesia and Thailand. In 1988, these countries accounted for less than 10 per cent of Nike's production. By 1992, this had increased to 44 per cent.

Not only was Nike able to move production rapidly in search of lower and lower costs, but it was also able to alter its global distribution network in response to world events. Clifford (1992) reports that Nike was faced by a potentially dangerous commercial threat in September and October 1992. Having moved much of the production of sports shoes to China, the US government became involved in a dispute with China over demands to open up the Chinese markets to American goods. The USA threatened to impose punitive tariffs on Chinese goods unless agreement was reached by October 10th. In response to this threat Nike planned to switch most of the output from Chinese factories to Europe. It also made an agreement with its Chinese suppliers that any loss resulting from any remaining shoes entering the US market would be split equally between Nike and the Chinese suppliers. In the end, the dispute was resolved and no action was needed.

Willigan (1992) emphasised how Nike developed its global marketing strategy in the late 1980s and early 1990s. One of Nike's major characteristics in marketing was the association of the product with the athlete: Michael Jordan with Air Jordan the basketball shoe, John McEnroe, Andre Agassi and Pete Sampras with tennis shoes and clothing. This association was an ideal way of marketing to a global market. The global media coverage of major sports events allowed Nike to establish a global marketplace for its products as this quote from Ian Hamilton, Nike's tennis marketing director, illustrates:

> When I started at Nike tennis, John McEnroe was the most visible player in the world, and he was already part of the Nike Family. He epitomised the type of player Nike wanted in its shoes – talented, dedicated, and loud. He broke racquets, drew fines, and, most of all, won matches. His success and behaviour drew attention on and off the court and put a lot of people in Nikes.
>
> (Willigan 1992: 95)

Similarly a further quote from Phil Knight stresses the importance of the association of the product with the athlete:

> The trick is to get athletes who not only can win but can stir up emotion. We want someone the public is going to love or hate, not just the leading scorer. To create a lasting emotional tie with consumers, we use the athletes repeatedly throughout their careers and present them as whole people.
>
> (Willigan 1992: 98)

Thus as John McEnroe got older and Andre Agassi replaced him as the fiery newcomer, Agassi became the promoter of Challenge Court, the exciting and colourful tennis range, while John McEnroe launched a new more subdued range, Supreme Court.

This policy of breaking down each individual sport into smaller and smaller sub-markets is another major characteristic of Nike's marketing approach. Thirty years ago, there was only one type of basketball shoe on the market and very few specialist running shoes. A trainer was an all-purpose sports shoe catering to a wide variety of sporting activities. Now there are different shoes and equipment for every sport. The Air Jordan basketball shoe was a concerted effort by Nike to create a completely new market for basketball shoes. It succeeded and later Nike further segmented the market with two other basketball shoe ranges, Flight and Force.

In the mid-1980s, Nike was losing out to Reebok, which was then the dominant force in the sports-shoe market. In 1987, Reebok had a 30 per cent market share of the US sports footwear market compared to Nike's 18 per cent. Nike's aggressive global marketing alongside its massive expenditure on athletes' endorsement contracts projected Nike way ahead of Reebok. By 1996, Nike had a 43 per cent share of the US footwear market while Reebok's share had dropped to 16 per cent. In the 1997 financial year alone, Nike increased its global revenue by 42 per cent to $9.2 billion (see Figure 5.1). Only three years earlier in 1994, Nike's global revenues stood at only $3.8 billion.

At this point in time Nike was spending over $1 billion annually on marketing and athlete endorsement contracts compared with a spend of around $400 million by Reebok. In January 1998, Reebok announced that it would no longer attempt to compete head-on with Nike any more largely because it could not match this massive investment in marketing its brand. Although Nike won the 'trainer wars' battle with Reebok, while it was going on, Adidas expanded in 1997 to become the second largest sports company in the world with global sales of over $5 billion spread across sports shoes, clothing, and equipment. Adidas had followed Nike in moving most of its manufacturing to Asia and aggressively marketing its brand with global advertising and athlete endorsement contracts.

However, things started to go wrong for Nike after its record-breaking 1996–7 financial results. As Naomi Klein, author of the book, *No Logo*, reports: Nike CEO Phil Knight has long been a hero of the business schools. Prestigious academic publications such as *The Harvard Business Review* have lauded his pioneering marketing techniques,

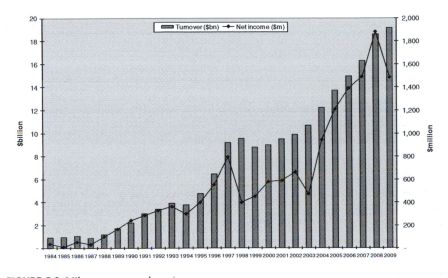

FIGURE 5.1 Nike turnover and net income
Source: Nike Annual Reports, various years

his understanding of branding and his early use of outsourcing. Countless MBA candidates and other students of marketing and communications have studied the Nike formula of 'brands not products'. So when Phil Knight was invited to be a guest speaker at the Stanford University Business School – Knight's own alma mater – in May 1997, the visit was expected to be one in a long line of Nike love-ins. Instead, Knight was greeted by a crowd of picketing students, and when he approached the microphone he was taunted with chants of 'Hey Phil, off the stage. Pay your workers a living wage'. The Nike honeymoon had come to a grinding halt.

No story illustrates the growing distrust of the culture of corporate branding more than the international anti-Nike movement, the most publicised and tenacious of the brand-based campaigns. Nike's sweatshop scandals have been the subject of over 1,500 news articles and opinion columns. Its Asian factories have been probed by cameras from nearly every major media organization, from CBS to Disney's sports station, ESPN (Klein 2000: 365–6).

Nike's problem was also the source of its financial success as Figure 5.2 illustrates. The 1990s Nike Air Carnivore retailing in the United States for $140 actually cost $4.40 in total labour cost. Chinese and Indonesian workers producing Nike's products were reported to earn $0.4 per hour. There were further allegations of use of child labour in Pakistan for sewing Nike footballs, and of sexual exploitation in factories producing Nike products.

Nike's initial response that it did not own these factories satisfied nobody. As Figure 5.1 shows, the long rise in Nike's turnover and profitability was reversed and Nike could not afford to ignore the protests. As Holmes (2004) indicates:

> When Nike was getting pummelled on the subject in the 1990s, it typically had only two responses: anger and panic. Executives would issue denials, lash

out at critics, and then rush someone to the offending supplier to put out the fire. But since 2002, Nike has built an elaborate program to deal with the charges of labour exploitation.

(Holmes 2004)

A new vice president for Corporate Responsibility was appointed and the first corporate responsibility report contained the admission that Nike knew far too little about what was happening in the factories and that its monitoring system was not working well enough.

By the end of the fiscal year ending May 2004, Nike was back on its growth trajectory. Its turnover shot up 15 per cent on the year before (see Figure 5.1), jumping from $10.7 billion to $12.3 billion. Its net income doubled from $474 million to $946 million. As Figure 5.1 indicates, this growth trajectory in turnover and net income then continued right through to the start of the global recession in 2008–9, with revenues peaking at $19.2 billion in 2009 and net income at $1.9 billion, both at almost double their 2004 values.

As Holmes (2004) indicates, this turnaround in financial performance was also associated with a turnaround in business approach: 'The New Nike … No longer the brat of sports marketing, it has a higher level of discipline and performance.' Nike even became official US Olympic sponsor for Beijing 2008 and 'toned down its anti-Establishment attitude' (Holmes 2004). The financial turnaround was not only brought about by greater emphasis on corporate responsibility, but also by greater concentration on global business performance.

Not everything has changed. Nike still invests up to 13 per cent of turnover in marketing. It still has 31 per cent of the global sports footwear market and this generates over half of its revenues. However, overseas sales are now larger and growing faster than US sales. Sales in China, for instance, increased by more than 50 per cent in 2009 alone, the year of the global recession.

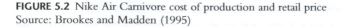

The Nike Air Carnivore

Retail Price	**$140**
Price at arrival in US	**$38.10**
Shipping	$1.40
Transport and Warehousing in SE Asia	$7.20
Ex factory	**$29.50**
Raw materials	$17.70
Labour cost	$4.40
Other costs	$7.40

FIGURE 5.2 Nike Air Carnivore cost of production and retail price
Source: Brookes and Madden (1995)

Transnational corporations in sport are not limited to producers or marketers of athletic goods (e.g. clothing, footwear, and equipment) but also now involve professional sports teams such as football clubs as well as media conglomerates that broadcast sport-related programming. The following case study of Real Madrid FC demonstrates how the organisation has gained the position of 'commercial leadership' in the global football market.

Real Madrid FC

Like other professional sports teams, Real Madrid's origins are not international; it is a Spanish club that competes primarily against other Spanish teams in domestic league and cup competitions in Spain. The few exceptions when Real Madrid plays outside its home country are in some UEFA matches (e.g. the European Champions League) and pre-season 'friendlies'.

During the 2000–2001 season, FIFA named Real Madrid the 'best soccer team of the 20th century'. This was a reflection of their dominance, both domestically and in Europe, during this period, when they won 31 *La Liga* titles, 18 Spanish *Copa del Rey* Cups, eight Spanish Super Cups, nine UEFA Champions Leagues, two UEFA Cups, one UEFA Supercup, as well as three Intercontinental Cups.

Regardless of their sporting dominance, when Florentino Pérez took over the club's presidency in 2000, Real Madrid was threatened by the most serious financial crisis in its history, as illustrated by Kexel (2010):

> Despite the fact that the team had won the European Champions League in 1998, the club was close to insolvency. Debts totalling €245 million exceeded the revenues of €118 million by more than 100 per cent, which resulted in an all time high operating loss of €65 million.
>
> Kexel (2010)

Yet, only five years later, Real Madrid's income grew by 200 per cent, reaching €276m, making it the wealthiest football club in the world at the expense of Manchester United (Deloitte 2006). Since then, Real Madrid has consistently maintained its number one ranking in terms of revenue generation year on year. In 2009, Real Madrid became the first sports team in the world to generate €400 million in revenues, which resulted in an operating profit of €93 million. Similarly, debts decreased to €120 million in the previous fiscal year leaving cash reserves of €112 million at the club's disposal (Deloitte 2010; Kexel 2010).

The remarkable turnaround in Real Madrid's fortunes is closely linked to its strategy of recruiting high profile players and those with a global following. In 2000, Real Madrid signed Luis Figo from rival club Barcelona for a then world record fee of €58.5 million and subsequently acquired Zinedine Zidane from Italian club Juventus in 2001 in a deal reportedly worth around €75 million (at current prices). Both Figo and Zidane were widely considered to be the best available players worldwide at the time. Then in 2002, Brazilian Ronaldo transferred from Inter Milan for €39 million;

however, it was the signing of David Beckham from Manchester United for €35 million in 2003 that first propelled Real Madrid to the top of Deloitte's 'football money league'. The acquisition of Beckham made sense for several reasons, giving Real Madrid a player with an enormous fan base cutting across all demographic, geographic, and socio-economic lines. Beckham, for instance, made his Real Madrid debut during a tour in Asia, where he was hugely popular, boosting the esteem of the club in an important market. Furthermore, Real Madrid, unlike most clubs, insisted upon retaining 50 per cent of the 'image rights' for each of its players, which meant that half of every endorsement deal Beckham signed as a Real Madrid player went to the club (Reference for Business 2011). Today, Real Madrid still holds this recruitment strategy dearly, which crystallises in the multi-million euro transfers in 2009 of Kaká (€65 million) and Cristiano Ronaldo (€93.5 million) from AC Milan and Manchester United respectively.

Ironically, the signing of these star players has failed to deliver the anticipated performance on the pitch. Real Madrid have won only two Spanish domestic league titles since 2000 and enjoyed little success in Europe – nonetheless, financial performance has continued to improve regardless of disappointment in terms of sporting success. This discrepancy can be explained by the tremendous increase in Real Madrid's commercial and broadcasting revenues, which totalled in excess of €300 million in 2010. Figure 5.3 illustrates that each source of revenue now separately exceeded the total revenues of 2000. Today, commercial and broadcasting revenues together represent more than 70 per cent of the total annual income.

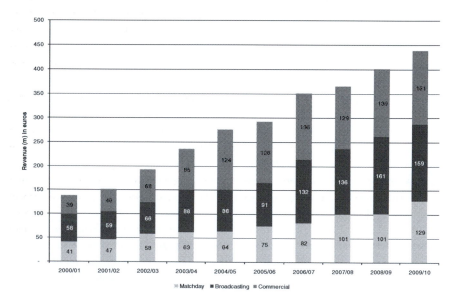

FIGURE 5.3 Real Madrid income and its sources
Source: Real Madrid Annual Reports, various years

These high earnings are a result of the club's strong domestic and international fan base. Indeed, the global appeal of the Real Madrid brand is highlighted by a recent study by Lipsman (2007) on the worldwide traffic to football websites. The study reported that Real Madrid attracted more than 1.1 million unique visitors to its website during March 2007, making it one of the world's most popular football clubs online. Perhaps more importantly, the study also showed that roughly two-thirds, or 760,000, of Real Madrid's million monthly visitors do not reside in Spain – quantifying the global reach and appeal of the Real Madrid brand franchise.

Such a global fan base allowed for the generation of €151m in its commercial revenues in 2010. Recruiting players, such as Beckham, Zidane and Ronaldo, has been the catalyst for substantial growth in merchandising and licensing revenues from Real Madrid's worldwide fan base. In 2004 and 2005, the team travelled to Asia for pre-season tours, building its support base and receiving lucrative appearance fees for matches in China, Japan and Thailand (Deloitte 2006). A TV–channel, named 'Real TV', reaching a total 200 million people worldwide in conjunction with an interactive TV-channel, was launched in 2005 being especially designed for Asia, which supports their successful endeavours. In addition, Real Madrid's website can be viewed in Spanish, English and Japanese (Kexel 2010).

The global commercial strategy of Real Madrid is also visible in their strategic alliances with companies operating worldwide. For example, since 2003 Real Madrid holds a strategic alliance with the car manufacturer Audi, thereby targeting the Asian market. Moreover in 2005 Real Madrid signed an agreement with the Chinese investment group 'CITIC Guon' in order to extend the club's profile in Asia by supporting Chinese youth teams. However, Kexel (2010) notes that Asia is not the only market Real Madrid has in mind: 'According to Real Madrid, fans outside of Europe are unprejudiced, thereby facilitating the acquisition of new fans. Due to this fact, the club announced a close partnership with Real Salt Lake, a club in US Major League Soccer.' According to BBDO Consulting, Real Madrid has the highest brand value among European soccer clubs, worth almost €1.1 billion, built through sponsorship and worldwide touring, including Asia, South America, and the United States (Bensch 2007).

Real Madrid's approach is sometimes criticised for being primarily commercially motivated rather than being driven by sporting success. It remains to be seen whether Real Madrid can reverse the trend of relatively modest on–pitch performances witnessed in recent times, just as they have managed to accomplish with their finances. Following on from Nike and Real Madrid, we now consider the case of Entertainment Sports Programming Network, or ESPN as it is more commonly known, and how it has established itself as the leading global sports media brand over the last two decades.

ESPN

Based in Bristol (Connecticut), USA, ESPN is 80 per cent owned by ABC, Inc., which is an indirect subsidiary of the Walt Disney Company. The Hearst Corporation holds a 20 per cent interest in ESPN (2011). Launched on 7 September 1979 by entrepreneur Bill Rasmussen, the company had already begun international distribution of its programming as early as April 1983. However, it was perhaps ESPN's live coverage of the America's Cup from Australia in 1987 that sparked the beginning of its expansion around the world. The company's push for globalisation is revealed by the following quote by Will Burkhardt of ESPN:

> ESPN entered the international marketplace because of a desire to grow out-side of the U.S. borders and to take what we had learned in the United States in terms of people's passion for sport ... and bring that to the international marketplace.
>
> (Czinkota and Ronkainen 2007: 645)

On 31 March 1989, ESPN International, a division of ESPN, launched its first net-work, in Latin America, which now transmits to 19 countries and territories, broad-casting in Spanish, Portuguese and English, and reaching over 33 million households in the region. ESPN entered Africa in June 1994 and currently serves 48 countries and 3.1 million homes via the leading television platform operator, Multichoice. In South Africa alone, ESPN reaches more than 1.5 million homes on television. In November 1996, ESPN entered into a 50:50 joint venture with STAR TV in Asia called ESPN STAR Sports. This collaboration reaches 310 million viewers in Asia, through 19 networks covering 24 countries, each localized to deliver differentiated world-class premier sports programming to Asian viewers. In 2002, ESPN launched its first bran-ded television channel in Europe, ESPN Classic, currently available in 23 million households in over 43 countries across Europe and can be seen in English, French, German, Italian, Polish, Portuguese, Turkish and Dutch. In February 2007, ESPN acquired NASN, the only European network dedicated to North American sports. The name of the network was re-branded to ESPN America in February 2009. The network airs over 800 live and as-live sports events each year, including those from the National Hockey League, the National Football League, Major League Baseball and NCAA. ESPN America is available in 14 million households, in over 43 Eur-opean countries (ESPN 2010a; ESPN 2010b; ESPN 2011). ESPN also operates net-works in Australia, New Zealand, the Middle East, Canada and the Caribbean. The net effect of these developments is that ESPN now owns 46 television networks ser-ving over 200 countries and territories across all seven continents in 16 languages (Cantonese, Dutch, English, French, German, Hindi, Italian, Japanese, Korean, Mandarin, Malay, Portuguese, Polish, Russian, Spanish and Turkish) (ESPN 2010a; ESPN 2011).

Cable television was still new when ESPN was founded and therefore not much data existed on who was watching what around the world, according to Boone and Kurtz (2010). But ESPN's executives had the idea that sports had universal appeal and decided to try broadcasting American sports events in South America. Today, South and Central America, particularly Argentina, Brazil and Mexico, represent 40 per cent of ESPN's total business (Boone and Kurtz 2010). Although the company continues to broadcast American sports overseas, the company's philosophy for global growth is to always serve sports fans and be locally relevant to them, with content and products that tap into their great passion and dedication (ESPN 2011). One of the most obvious examples of this type of localised approach, in terms of tailoring its programmes to specific audiences, is the sheer volume of cricket coverage delivered by ESPN STAR Sports in the Indian market, including a dedicated cricket channel (STAR Cricket). While few Americans are familiar with the sport, millions of Indians are glued to the TV for cricket matches. Similarly, in Argentina, rugby and polo occupy prime time coverage (Boone and Kurtz 2010). In Europe, ESPN Classic shows soccer, rugby and cricket compared to the American version which shows a lot of football, basketball and baseball. George Bodenheimer, President of ESPN Inc., explains how ESPN has adopted a two-pronged strategy on the international front:

> First, we take successful models of ESPN franchises and expand and adapt them abroad. We have created locally tailored versions of ESPN Classic, Sports-Center, the X Games and ESPN The Magazine in a number of markets. Second, while we build on our North American sports expertise, we work with rights holders on the most popular local sports around the world – whether it is live cricket and soccer through ESPN STAR in Asia, or the UEFA Champions League in Africa, Latin America, Australia and the US.
>
> (Sport Business 2008)

Despite its fan-centric approach to driving media expansion, ESPN starts with a regional marketing strategy, 'building a bed of programming from which you then start to localize' (Czinkota and Ronkainen 2007). However, the methods used by ESPN to enter international markets are varied, as explained by Boone and Kurtz (2010):

> In Europe, ESPN has had a longstanding partnership with Eurosport, which means that although many European consumers watch sports on cable televi-sion, they are not necessarily aware of the ESPN name. ESPN operates in Canada through partnerships as well. These arrangements are partly due to varying regulations in varying countries and regions. But in Asia, ESPN has a large operation of its own, broadcasting to about 25 countries on the continent, including India, which is one of the firm's most important markets.
>
> (Boone and Kurtz 2010)

The strength of ESPN has been its ability to recognise the need to identify, even create trends in the world of sports (Gitman and McDaniel 2009). Not only does ESPN broadcast sport-related programming around the globe, it often acts as a promoter and event manager, most notably in the case of *X Games*, the world's premier action sports competition, which is staged throughout the world. In addition to the two US-based events, ESPN has held *X Games* competitions and demonstration events around the world including Brazil, China, Japan, Dubai, Singapore, Taiwan, the

Philippines, UAB, France, Korea, Malaysia, Mexico, Spain and Thailand. In March 2010, ESPN launched Winter X Games Europe in Tignes, France, the first *Winter X Games* event outside of the US (ESPN 2011). Audiences can either see events live in an arena, on TV, or across a number of multimedia platforms, including broadband, mobile video and iPods (Sport Business 2008).

ESPN's expansion and worldwide presence has not been limited to just television channels; it has also experimented with alternative broadcast platforms, as emphasised by George Bodenheimer:

> We're not just in the TV business anymore ... We're going to the table as a sports media company. We've been approaching our business this way for 10 years now, and have learned that fans want sports content when and where they want it, regardless of platform.
>
> (Sport Business 2008)

For example, ESPN operates an industry-leading portfolio of websites, including UK based ESPNsoccernet.com, which is one of the most popular football websites in the world, reaching over four million unique users a month in more than 100 countries with the latest football news, scores and features. The site is available in English, French, German, Spanish and Italian. In 2007, ESPN acquired Cricinfo.com, the world's leading cricket website and Scrum.com, a leading rugby news information site. Cricinfo.com now reaches more than seven million users every month and it is ranked number one in all of its major markets. Scrum.com has established a strong and growing presence among worldwide rugby fans since its inception (ESPN 2010b; ESPN 2011). In August 2008, ESPN acquired Racing-Live.com, the world's leading independent motor racing website, which provides fans around the world with locally tailored news and information in English, French, Japanese, Italian, German and Spanish. Racing-Live.com has earned a devoted fan base of three million unique users per month. ESPN has subsequently launched a re-branded and re-designed site – ESPNF1.com – in January 2010. In August 2010, ESPN in the UK launched ESPN Goals, a comprehensive mobile football service delivering live video, scores and news. ESPN Goals is the first place for football fans to see video of all the goals and highlights for all Barclays Premier League matches each week over the next three seasons – within minutes of the action on the pitch (ESPN 2010b; ESPN 2011).

Bodenheimer notes that 'growing our media options also strengthens our brand – particularly among younger fans that are most prone to use new media options.' ESPN's success in the mobile market also lends support to this view. As of July 2008, ESPN Mobile reported a 78 per cent increase in year-to-year traffic, and was the top-rated mobile sports site and seventh site overall in mobile web, according to Sport Business (2008).

Conclusions

The Nike, Real Madrid and ESPN case studies show a model of the growth of global sports corporations through the development of a worldwide demand for a given product. It is a model where growth can be sustained through continual expansion of demand. Demand expansion is sustained by the creation of new geographic markets. The new emerging markets, such as China and India, with one-third of the world's population, have provided huge opportunities for these global sports corporations. As sections of these economies have become richer, the market for sport has expanded at a huge rate. Thus Nike increased its sales in China by 50 per cent in 2009 alone. At some point Penrose's constraints on growth of demand will also affect global demand but that will be sometime long into the future.

6

SPORT BROADCASTING

Introduction

Over the last two decades, perhaps the most striking development in the sport industry has been the rapid evolution of the broadcast demand for sport. The demand for sports broadcasting can be expressed in two ways. First, for media companies this refers to the ever-increasing competition for, and willingness to transmit, sport-related programming, primarily through the coverage of live sport. In return for such coverage broadcasters are required to pay the requisite fees to the owners of the broadcast rights. Second, for the ordinary sports fan the demand for sports broadcasting is essentially the demand to watch live broadcasts of sport.

In the case of major sports events, the costs for sports fans associated with attending a live event can be exceedingly high. The total cost here will include, for example, tickets, travel to and from the venue, food and drink and sometimes accommodation associated with the trip. To illustrate this point, the average (median) expenditure excluding tickets by spectators across 16 major sports events held in the UK between 1997 and 2003 was found to be almost £50 per person per day (UK Sport 2004). Moreover, the cost of attending a top flight football match in England has jumped by about 600 per cent since 1989 (Ornstein and Soneji 2008).

On the other hand, if the event is broadcast live, then watching the event on television may provide a substantially cheaper alternative. Increasingly, watching sport on television will require the fan to pay for the privilege through a pay-per-view channel. Even then, the total cost of watching sport will normally be substantially cheaper than attending a live event.

Irrespective of the definition adopted, the demand for sports broadcasting reaches its highest point where genuine global sports events are involved. This has, in turn, led to a significant escalation in the prices of broadcasting rights for such events. The increases in rights fees are way above the rate of inflation. A number of contributing factors have impacted on their burgeoning growth but primarily the satellite and digital broadcasting revolution is responsible. New distribution methods and broadcasting platforms, including satellite TV, cable TV, internet TV, interactive TV, digital TV and broadband cable have arisen during this growth period and, crucially, all need premium content to drive subscriptions to their new services. These broadcasters need desirable, exclusive content that will distinguish them from their competitors. Elite sporting properties fit into this category. Hence, the most powerful sports rights holders, those with consistently large and proven audiences, have seen the value of their most prized intellectual property – live broadcasting rights – become the target of frenzied media rights battles during this growth period (Clarke 2002).

Nonetheless, Clarke (2002) argues that only a finite number of sports, primarily soccer in Europe and the big four – basketball, American football, baseball and ice hockey – in the US, together with global sporting events such as the FIFA World Cup and the Olympics have seen their rights fees explode. Many other sports have experienced marked increases in their rights fees during this period as broadcasters seek to expand their sports portfolios and fill the schedules of newly launched sports channels, but it is those elite sporting events that pay-TV companies regard as 'must see' television for which values have risen most sharply. It is these properties, particularly those with season-long schedules, that broadcasters believe will persuade consumers to take out subscriptions to their services. Often during this growth period, pay-TV companies have been prepared to pay very large sums for exclusive live broadcasting rights fees fully aware that this money cannot be reimbursed through advertising and sponsorship sold around the sporting event(s). In many territories, these sporting properties have served as loss leaders for the broadcasters as they drive subscriptions whilst simultaneously preventing competitors from doing likewise (Clarke 2002).

However, even for those 'protected' sporting events deemed to be of such national importance that they can only be sold to terrestrial broadcasters and are therefore not directly affected by the growth of pay-TV broadcasters, rights fees have still grown. To an extent, this has been merely a re-alignment of rights fees. Broadcasters were making huge profits from the acquisition of elite sporting events a decade and more ago. The power has shifted towards the intellectual property holders who have grown aware of the importance and value of their sports properties (Clarke 2002).

In this chapter, we consider these developments in the context of two events of global sporting significance – the Olympic Games and the Football World Cup. Both the IOC and FIFA have a membership of over 200 national associations, which is more than the United Nations and which serves to demonstrate their global appeal. This chapter also looks in detail at the English Premier League as an example of how a domestic sporting competition can become a global broadcast product.

Broadcast rights for sports properties

According to TV Sports Markets' second annual survey (Sport Business 2010a), the top 10 properties now all bring in over $1 billion per annum in television-rights fees – see Table 6.1.

TABLE 6.1 Top 10 sports properties by global TV income

	Property	Duration	Years	Estimated fee p.a. ($bn)
1	NFL	2006 to 2013	8	3.86
2	Summer Olympics (London)	2012	1	2.50
3	2010 Fifa World Cup	2010	1	2.19
4	2014 Fifa World Cup	2014	1	2.50
5	English Premier League	2007–8 to 2009–10	3	1.64
6	Italian Serie A	2010–11 to 2015–16	6	1.32
7	Winter Olympics (Vancouver)	2010	1	1.30
8	UEFA Champions League	2009–10 to 2011–12	3	1.23
9	NBA	2008–09 to 2015–16	8	1.03
10	French Ligue 1	2008–09 to 2011–12	4	1.01

Source: TV Sports Markets
Notes:
2014 World Cup: deals yet to be concluded in Spain and sub-Saharan Africa
2010 and 2012 Olympics: Latin America (excluding Brazil), free-to-air rights in sub-Saharan Africa

In terms of global television revenue, American football's National Football League (NFL) brings in more revenue from television rights sales than any other rights-holder. Recent extensions with its incumbent domestic broadcasters mean it now brings in an estimated average of $3.855 billion per annum in rights fees until 2011. The extension agreed with network partners CBS, Fox and NBC brings them into line with cable sports channel ESPN expiring in 2013. But thanks to a new deal with its other domestic partner DirecTV, it will now bring in $4.074 billion a year in those two years – the NFL negotiating a 43 per cent increase in rights fee with DirecTV.

The 2012 Olympic Games is the second-biggest television property and a recent deal with state broadcaster CCTV in China boosted the running total for the event to $2.5 billion, with the International Olympic Committee still to do deals in Latin America (excluding Brazil) and sub-Saharan Africa (for free-to-air rights only). The stunning success of CCTV's coverage of the Beijing Olympics in 2008 paved the way for a record television rights deal for the 2010 and 2012 Games. CCTV is paying $100 million for the multi-platform rights for 2010 and 2012 (of which $82 million is for the London Games), approximately 450 per cent more than it paid for the 2006 and 2008 Games. It is China's biggest ever television sports rights deal. The IOC has already begun its sales process for the 2014 and 2016 Olympic Games, with the Sportfive agency agreeing deals in Korea and Turkey, plus a large number of European markets. Its deals in Brazil, which were agreed just weeks before the announcement that Rio de Janeiro would host the 2016 Games, brought in $170 million, more than three times what was paid for 2008 and 2010. In total, the IOC has brought in close to $950 million for the 2014 and 2016 Games so far.

Another rights holder which is well into its negotiations for its next contract period is the English Premier League. The league brought in $1.64 billion per year in global television rights fees over the 2007–8 to 2009–10 period. Early deals for 2010–11 to

2012–13 point to a big increase for the league. Not only did it secure a 4.5 per cent increase in fees for its domestic live rights, it has brought in massive increases in revenue from other parts of the world. In the Middle East, it tripled its take after signing a deal with the Abu Dhabi Media Company. A similar rise was achieved in India and in both Singapore and Malaysia fees have increased by 70 per cent.

Domestic football leagues are the lifeblood of pay-television companies all around Europe. Of the top 10 single deals in the region, seven are between national leagues and pay-operators. The high cost and limited opportunity of supporting a team at the stadium means there is a massive demand from fans to watch their favourite team on television. This in turn is a key driver of pay-television subscriptions and explains the massive fees paid by subscription-based companies. For the same reason, in Latin America, football leagues attract the highest rights fees. National leagues in other sports attract the top fees in other parts of the world. In the USA, the NFL, the NBA, the NCAA and the MLB leagues all attract massive fees. In Asia-Pacific, the domestic deal in India for the Indian Premier League is the second biggest agreement in the region. Deals in Australia for the AFL and NRL also rank high.

A feature of the global market for sports broadcasting is that it operates under imperfect competition. It all depends on whether the market is in short supply (excess demand) or short demand (excess supply). The short side of the market usually imposes its transaction conditions on those competing together on the long side of the market. Andreff (2008) identifies four different forms of the sports broadcasting market, as follows:

a) A *monopoly* when only one organiser supplies his/her exclusive sports event to competing TV channels (consider the IOC offering the Olympic Games, FIFA with the football World Cup). In a monopoly market, price is relatively high, broadcasting rights expensive, and revenues accruing to the organiser big.

b) An *oligopolistic monopoly* when only one event organiser is facing very few potential buyers – TV channels (UEFA Champions League, French football championships). Broadcasting rights are still high though lower than in the monopoly case due to fewer competitors on the demand side.

c) A *bilateral monopoly* when a single public TV channel monopolises the demand side of a domestic market or when a European cartel of public channels (ERU) merged all demands for a sports event to be broadcast on a European scale. In the case of bilateral monopoly, economic theory teaches that the transaction price is determined by the relative bargaining power (not necessarily economic or financial) of the monopoly and the monopsony. Usually the price is lower than the price emerging in the presence of a pure or oligopolistic monopoly.

d) A *monopsony* when professional clubs are competing for the sale of their individual broadcasting rights to a single TV channel (French football championship in the 1970s) instead of the league pooling the rights for all clubs. Then, in such a case, the lowest price is reached, as well as the lowest revenues for sports organisers, since they are competing on the long side of the market in the face of a single buyer.

Theoretical issues

Why has sport seen such an escalation in the price of broadcasting rights? Todreas (1999) provides a possible explanation that relates more to the development of the television industry than that of the sport industry. His explanation is mainly in the context of the US market. Todreas points to the supply chain of television programmes which consists of 'content' and 'conduit'. 'Conduit' refers to the distribution of programmes to consumers by the television companies. He refers to this as the downstream end of the supply chain. 'Content' consists of the upstream suppliers, in our case the teams and leagues that produce sports contests. As television markets have developed, he argues that value 'migrates upsteam', that is profitability switches from the owners of the conduit to the owners of the content.

To explain this, he identifies three eras in the history of television: the broadcast era (for the USA, late 1940s to early 1970s); the cable era (early 1970s to early 1990s); and the digital era (early 1990s to the present). He argues that in the broadcast era, it was the television stations that owned the conduit that were highly profitable because of their monopoly power. There were few suppliers and these tended not to compete directly with each other but rather operate more as a cartel. The cable era saw some expansion of operators at the conduit end of the supply chain, but cable licences were restricted with often only one granted for each municipality.

The digital era, however, brought in new competitors in the distribution of programmes and new ways (e.g. telephone, internet) of distributing content. This new competition reduced margins and profits, destroyed value in the conduit and increased value in the content. The new technology changed the methods of distribution but it did not change the process of content creation. Sports teams and leagues supplying content were in a strong bargaining position. There was increased competition for the limited supply of sport content.

If this was the situation in the USA, the situation was even more favourable for sports content owners in new markets targeted by the new generation of broadcasters. Sports programmes almost uniquely had this ability to attract the size and characteristics of audiences most attractive to distributors, sponsors and advertisers. These audiences were also willing to pay a premium price to broadcasters to receive more of the sports content than had been previously supplied by the old free-to-air networks. As these developments were taking place, in Europe in particular, governments were stepping back from the old regulatory distribution systems and liberalising television in order to encourage the development of the new digital technology. However, it was not long before these same governments stepped in to regulate what they perceived to be the adverse effects on sports broadcasting from the new television landscape.

Although the escalation in the price of broadcasting rights for sports events and leagues is the single largest development in the sports broadcasting market, it is not the only one. In 1964, CBS bought the New York Yankees for $14 million. In 1965, Jack Kent Cooke, a cable TV operator, bought the Los Angeles Lakers and a year later the Los Angeles Kings. Although CBS and Cooke resold these franchises in the 1970s, these episodes signalled the beginnings of a closer relationship between television companies and professional sports teams in the USA that was to be become more common both in the USA and globally in later years.

In more recent times, we have seen the growth in what has been called the 'global mass media oligopoly' (Law *et al.* 2002) including AOL-Time Warner, Bertelsmann, Disney Corporation, News Corporation, Viacom and Vivendi-Universal. In many of these global media giants, sport has played an important role. AOL-Time Warner owns the Atlantic Hawks of the NBA and the Atlanta Braves of the NL. Disney Corporation, which owns ABC and ESPN, own the NHL team, the Anaheim Ducks.

Perhaps the strongest relationship between sport and global media expansion, however, is that of Rupert Murdoch's News Corporation. Andrews (2003) analysed how News Corporation used sport as an instrument for successfully penetrating national television markets within the United States, the United Kingdom, Asia and Australasia. Fox did this by acquiring sports broadcasting rights in the USA and BSkyB did the same in the UK. Similar tactics were achieved by Foxtel in Australia, JSkyB in Japan, Zee TV in India, and Sky in New Zealand. In most of these cases (the main exception being Fox in the USA), the News Corporation channel was introduced as a pay-per-view channel, with sports prominent, into markets conventionally used to sport being predominantly on free-to-air public service broadcasting.

Broadcasting and the Olympics

The IOC is the owner of the broadcast rights, including television, mobile and internet, for the Olympic Summer Games and Olympic Winter Games. The IOC is responsible for allocating Olympic broadcast rights to media companies throughout the world through the negotiation of rights agreements. The television broadcast of the Olympic Games and the Olympic Winter Games is the most significant factor in the communication of the Olympic ideals worldwide. Television rights to the Olympic Games are sold principally to broadcasters that can guarantee the broadest coverage throughout their respective territories.

The primary broadcasting objective of the Olympic Movement is to ensure that most television viewers possible have the opportunity to experience the Olympic Games. In pursuit of this objective, coverage of the Olympic Games has been made available in an increasing number of nations, territories and markets throughout the world. Global Olympic broadcast audience and viewer figures continue to rise as the Olympic broadcast spreads to more nations and territories, as more viewers throughout the world gain access to television, and as the appeal of Olympic Games programming continues to grow – see Table 6.2.

Olympic broadcast programming is generated by the Olympic host broadcast organisation, which captures the television and radio signal from each Olympic venue and delivers the signal to the Olympic broadcast partners to air over various media platforms throughout the world. With increased capability and technological sophistication, the host broadcaster has greatly expanded its live feed of Olympic competition and ceremonial action in recent decades. Beginning in 2009, the Olympic Broadcast

TABLE 6.2 Television coverage and global audience of the Olympic Games 1992–2008

Year	Number of nations	Host broadcaster feed (hours)	Global coverage (hours)	Cumulative audience (billion)*	Total viewer hours (billion)**	Average minute rating (million)***	Viewer reach (billion)
Summer Olympics							
Barcelona 1992	193	2,800	20,000	16.6	n/a	n/a	Unavailable
Atlanta 1996	214	3,000	25,000	19.6	33.5	n/a	Unavailable
Sydney 2000	220	3,500	29,600	n/a	33.2	113.5	3.7
Athens 2004	220	3,800	43,800	n/a	34.4	78.0	3.9
Beijing 2008	220	5,000	61,700	n/a	Unavailable	160.0	4.3
Winter Olympics							
Albertville 1992	86	350	Unavailable	8.0	n/a	Unavailable	Unavailable
Lillehammer 1994	120	331	Unavailable	10.7	n/a	Unavailable	Unavailable
Nagano 1998	160	600	Unavailable	10.7	11.6	Unavailable	Unavailable
Salt Lake City 2002	160	900	10,416	n/a	13.1	Unavailable	2.1
Turin 2006	200	1,000	16,311	n/a	10.6	Unavailable	3.1

Note on broadcast viewer measurement:
The IOC has modified its approach to measuring the global audience of the Olympic broadcast from cumulative audience or Total Total Viewer Hours to Average Minute Rating (AMR). This shift in methodology is designed to provide greater accuracy in determining the appeal of Olympic television programming throughout the world.

* *Cumulative audience* is derived by determining the aggregate number of times each television viewer around the world tuned in to Olympic Games television programming.

** *Total viewer hours* measures the number of hours of Olympic programming that have captured the attention of the global television viewing audience during the Olympic Games. Viewer hours per programme are measured by multiplying the duration of the programme by the number of viewers in the audience. Total viewer hours for the Olympic Games and Olympic Winter Games are the sum of all viewer hours per programme.

*** *Average minute rating* measures the number of viewers watching a typical minute of Olympic Games television coverage. The global figure is calculated by combining the average minute rating of dedicated Games coverage aired by official broadcasters.

Services (OBS) (a company wholly owned by the IOC) oversees the host broadcaster function for the Games. OBS was formed by the IOC to serve as the permanent host broadcast organisation for both the Summer and Winter Games.

From the full range of available material, each Olympic broadcast partner may select the particular events that it will include in its schedule of Olympic programming. Each Olympic broadcast partner has the opportunity to deliver those events and images that it determines to be of greatest interest to the target audience in its home country or territory. The events that are aired in the Olympic programming of one broadcast partner are not necessarily the events that are aired by another broadcast partner.

Increased host broadcast coverage has afforded the Olympic broadcast partners greater programming opportunities in more sports and enabled the broadcast partners to deliver more complete Olympic coverage to their audiences around the world. The IOC works in partnership with its broadcasters to ensure that an increasing amount of live coverage is available, and that the latest technologies, including HDTV, live coverage on the internet and coverage on mobile phones is available in as many territories as possible.

Olympic broadcast partnerships have provided the Olympic Movement with an unprecedented financial base and helped to ensure the future viability of the Olympic Games. The global broadcast revenue figure for the 2008 Olympic Games in Beijing represents a threefold increase from the 1992 Barcelona broadcast revenue less than two decades earlier. Similarly, the global broadcast revenue figure for the 2006 Olympic Winter Games in Turin also represents a threefold increase from the 1992 Albertville broadcast revenue less than two decades earlier – see Figure 6.1.

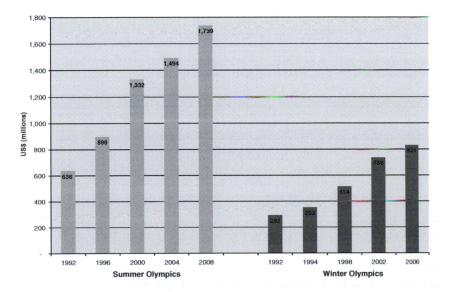

FIGURE 6.1 Olympic broadcast revenue generation 1992–2008

TABLE 6.3 Latest 2010–12 Olympic broadcast rights fee

Region/territory	Broadcaster	Rights fee (US$m)
USA	NBC	2,000.00
Canada	CTV	153.00
Brazil	Record	60.00
Rest of Latin America	ESPN/Terra	17.50
Caribbean	IMC	0.75
Americas' sub-total		2,231.25
China	CCTV	99.50
Japan	JC	355.90[1]
Korea	SBS	33.00
Philippines	Solar	2.00
Hong Kong	i-Cable	14.88
Rest of Asia	ABU/ESPN Star	15.25
Chinese Taipei	Elta	0.09
Asia sub-total		520.62
Arab states	ASBU/ART	21.20
South Africa	SABC	16.00
Sub-Saharan Africa	SABC	2.00
Middle East / Africa sub-total		39.20
Italy	Sky Italia	152.30[2]
Europe	EBU	761.40[3]
Europe sub-total		913.70
Australia	Nine	113.20[4]
New Zealand	Sky Network	10.50
Oceania sub-total		123.70
Total		3,828.47

Notes:
[1] JPY 32.5 trillion
[2] €112 million
[3] €560 million
[4] AU$ 126 million

The collective global value of the latest 2010 Vancouver Winter Games and 2012 London Summer Games broadcast rights fee is estimated to be around US$3.83 billion – see Table 6.3. This figure is US$ 1,258 million (or almost 1.5 times) greater than the cumulative broadcast revenue earned from the 2006 and 2008 Olympics.

Olympic broadcast partnerships have been the single greatest source of revenue for the Olympic Movement for more than three decades. The Olympic Movement generates revenue through six major programmes. The IOC manages broadcast partnerships, the TOP worldwide sponsorship programme and the IOC official supplier and licensing programme. The OCOGs manage domestic sponsorship, ticketing and licensing programmes within the host country, under the direction of the IOC. Figure 6.2 provides details of the total revenue generated from each major programme managed by the IOC and the OCOGs during the past four Olympic quadrenniums.

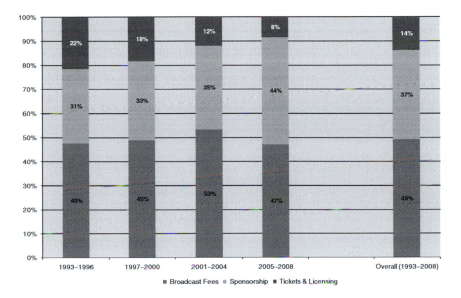

FIGURE 6.2 Olympic broadcast revenue in context

During the period 1993–2008, broadcast fees have contributed at least 47 per cent of the total Olympic marketing revenue and on average account for nearly half (49 per cent) of all revenue generated. Meanwhile, sponsorship (including both the TOP programme and domestic sponsorship) and tickets and licensing were respectively responsible for 37 per cent and 14 per cent of total marketing revenue between 1993 and 2008. Such figures serve to highlight the relative importance of broadcast revenues to the financial well-being of the Olympics.

The Football World Cup

Similar to the Olympic Games, analysis of broadcast data on the Football World Cup reveals a pattern of increases in the supply of television coverage, the number of global television viewers, and the broadcast rights fees secured over the past five editions of the event – see Table 6.4.

TABLE 6.4 Key broadcast statistics for the FIFA World Cup 1990–2006

Year	Broadcast countries	Total transmission time (hrs)	Cumulative TV audience (bn)	TV rights (SFr. m)
Italy 1990	167	14,693	26.69	95
USA 1994	188	16,393	32.12	110
France 1998	196	29,145	24.77	135
Japan/South Korea 2002	213	41,324	28.84	1,300
Germany 2006	214	73,072	26.29	1,500

Television coverage of the 2006 World Cup in Germany was the most extensive to date with 376 channels showing the event (compared to 232 in 2002). Furthermore, the 2006 event was aired in a total of 43,600 broadcasts across 214 countries and territories, generating total coverage in excess of 73,000 hours. The Football World Cup is commonly described by FIFA as 'world's no. 1 sports event'. Independent audience research conducted on behalf of potential sponsors and advertisers has confirmed the competition's status as the world's most popular event by revealing that the 2006 World Cup Final between Italy and France was the most viewed sports event on television in 2006, attracting 607.9 million in-home viewers, 'more than twice as many viewers as any other program' (Cone 2006). The international appeal of the tournament was illustrated by the fact that more people in China tuned into the England versus Paraguay game than the entire populations of England and Paraguay. The match was broadcast in China on CCTV-5 at 9 p.m., attracting 62.9 million viewers, with 22.3 per cent of China's television viewers at that time choosing to watch the match (Sport Business 2006).

The global appeal of the Football World Cup can be further appreciated by taking into consideration the breakdown of viewers of the 2006 event by broad geographic region as shown in Figure 6.3. The figures quite clearly illustrate that the distribution of viewer numbers is broadly in line with what one might expect given the relative population of each territory. For example, Asia is ranked first in terms of population and also in terms of viewers. The figures also confirm the stature of the World Cup (and football in general) in Europe, which is ranked third in terms of population but second in terms of viewership.

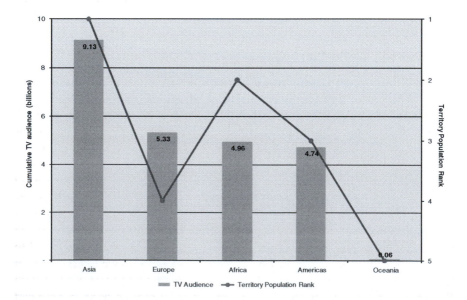

FIGURE 6.3 2006 FIFA World Cup TV audiences by territory (evidence of global appeal)

The cumulative television audience figure, as reported by FIFA, for the 2006 World Cup was 26.29 billion (comprising 24.2 billion in-home and 2.1 billion out-of-home viewers). This represents an increase in viewers on the 1998 event, which like 2006 was also staged in Europe, but is a little below the 28.84 billion viewers for the 2002 event. The drop in cumulative audience numbers in 2006 relative to 2002 can be primarily attributed to the reduction in viewing in Asia, which fell by 25.7 per cent from 11.16 billion in 2002 to 8.28 billion in 2006. This, however, does not necessarily indicate a reduction in public interest for watching the Football World Cup amongst viewers in Asia. Rather, there are two factors that help to explain the figures. First, the 2002 World Cup was staged in two Asian territories (Japan and South Korea) and kick-off times for live matches were consequently during prime viewing hours across most of the region, whereas live matches in 2006 were shown mostly after midnight. Second, China (which accounts for approximately one-fifth of the total global audience) qualified for the event proper for a historic first time in 2002 but failed to do so in 2006. Such circumstances explain the 9 per cent fall in global cumulative audience in 2006.

Despite the fluctuations in television audience figures for the World Cup over time, the value of broadcasting rights continues to rise year on year. Revenue from the sale of television broadcast rights between 1990 and 1998 steadily increased from 95 million Swiss Francs in 1990 to 135 million Swiss Francs in 1998. The three competitions – 1990, 1994 and 1998 – sold to a consortium of mainly public broadcasters for a total of 340 million Swiss Francs. However, there was a phenomenal rise in the value of television rights for the 2002 and 2006 World Cups which were sold to Kirch of Germany for 1.3 billion Swiss Francs and 1.5 billion Swiss Francs respectively. It is reported (at the time of writing) that FIFA will net about 25 billion rand (US$2.8 million) from the sale of television rights to broadcast the 2010 World Cup in South Africa. This figure exceeds the broadcast revenue FIFA received for the past two World Cups combined.

Listed events

This section will focus on direct regulations in sports broadcasting that regulate which channels are allowed to broadcast specific sports events. Examples of such regulations are the European *Listed Events* legislation and the Australian *Anti-Siphoning List*, which prevent pay-TV channels from broadcasting events that are of special value for society. All countries that have listed events legislation include at least some part of the summer Olympic Games and the football World Cup on their lists. This legislation is a reaction to the tendency seen in many countries for the top sports events only to be shown live on pay TV with the free-to-air channels restricted to showing edited highlights. It dates back to the 1990s when many pay TV providers started to concentrate on sport content to expand their subscription base as we have seen earlier in the chapter. A consequence of this development was that governments in both Europe and Australia implemented regulations that define sports programmes as a part of the public domain. Late in the 1990s, so-called *Listed Events Regulations* were established in several European countries, while the *Australian Anti-siphoning List* was launched in the mid-1990s.

The main criterion for listing in the UK was that the event has a special national resonance, not just a significance to those who ordinarily follow the sport concerned; it is an event which serves to unite the nation, a shared point on the national calendar. For a sporting event, it would also fall into one or both of the following categories:

- it is a pre-eminent national or international event in the sport;
- it involves the national team or national representatives in the sport concerned.

Effectively, in economic terms, it would mean that the event had the potential to generate the public good benefits of international sporting success, the argument being that if such an event were only broadcast on pay TV, major sections of the population would be excluded from these public good benefits.

The governing body that owns the rights to the event has a dilemma. By selling to a pay-TV broadcaster with limited penetration they maximise revenue but reduce the exposure of the event to the public. At the same time, this reduces the attractiveness of the event to sponsors who want maximum exposure. Ideally, governing bodies want maximum exposure of their sport and the highest revenue but achieving both of these objectives is not possible. In general, the higher the revenue achieved from the sale of the broadcasting rights the lower the exposure. If the event is listed, the choice is no longer with the governing body. It is with the government who decide to give the event maximum exposure. The cost is reduced revenue to the governing body. The main case against listing is that governing bodies argue that they know more about their own sport than anybody else and that they are in the best position to make the decision as to who to sell the broadcasting rights to. Listed events legislation is the one area where governments can have some control over the monopoly power of the GSOs.

In 2009, the UK government set up an Independent Advisory Panel (IAP) to review the listed events legislation. This panel received evidence from broadcasters, national and international governing bodies of sport and media experts over a four-month period and it is interesting to look at some of that evidence, in particular from the IOC and FIFA, to reveal just how important to the GSOs such government intervention is.

The IOC argued that it had always tried to achieve the widest possible dissemination of images of the Olympic Games in line with the Olympic Charter, which requires that the IOC take 'all necessary steps in order to ensure the fullest coverage by the different media and the widest possible audience in the world for the Olympic Games'. In general then, this requires the IOC to sell the broadcasting rights to free-to-air broadcasters.

However, although the IOC is happy for all those parts of the Olympics that are of significant importance to the UK viewing public to be shown on terrestrial television and even be listed, it objects to the whole of the Olympic Games being listed. The argument is quite straightforward. At the Beijing Olympics, live Olympic Games content amounted to 5,000 hours covering 28 sports. To broadcast all 5,000 hours live would require at least 26 channels broadcasting 12 hours a day for the 16 days of the Olympics. In fact the BBC, the owner of the UK broadcast rights to the Beijing Olympics, broadcast 240 hours of live content from Beijing or just 4.8 per cent of the total. That is, 95 per cent of the Olympic Games content was not broadcast to the UK viewing public.

The IOC argued that the current UK listing arrangements, where the whole of the Olympic Games is listed, are detrimental to Olympic sports, some of which get no coverage at all by the BBC, and to the host cities and National Olympic Committees, who receive 92 per cent of all the Olympic Games marketing revenues. Quite simply, the IOC would like a form of listing which allows the BBC, or any other terrestrial broadcaster, to broadcast that content most demanded by the UK viewers, but preserves the right of the IOC to market the remaining live content to other broadcasters.

FIFA's argument in relation to the World Cup was similar in that they were happy for part of the tournament to be listed (e.g. opening match, matches of home nations, semi-finals, and final) but they preferred a model operated in some other European countries (e.g. France) where a partnership between free-to-air and pay TV broadcasters shared the tournament. The IOC argument focussed on the lack of coverage of live Olympic content. This was not the case with the World Cup, however, as all matches are currently shown live. It was the loss of broadcast revenue that was FIFA's main concern. In 2007, event income accounted for 89 per cent of FIFA revenue with the bulk of this coming from the sale of broadcasting rights to the 2010 World Cup (DCMS 2009). FIFA's objective is clearly to increase that revenue by reducing government control of its sale of the broadcasting rights for the World Cup, in particular by allowing pay TV providers to enter the market.

The English Premier League

The English Premier League does not suffer from such government interference in the sale of its broadcasting rights since domestic football matches are not able to meet the 'national resonance' criteria. The Premier League was formed in 1992 when the 22 First Division (as it was then) clubs resigned from the Football League and set up their own division in order to attract greater revenue from television (Bevan and Stevenson 2008). The number of clubs in the Premier League has since been capped at twenty. At the time of writing this chapter, there have been 17 completed seasons of the Premier League.

Evidence of domestic appeal

Since its inception, the Premier League has been an unprecedented success in the UK. Table 6.5 summarises the attendance figures for Premier League matches for the 2008–9 season. The aggregate attendance across the 380 games played was more than 13.5 million. Thus, on average, there were 35,663 people who attended a Premier

TABLE 6.5 Premier League attendances for the 2008–9 season

Club	Home games	Aggregate attendance	Average attendance	Capacity	Utilisation	Final league position
Manchester United	19	1,430,866	75,309	76,180	99%	1
Liverpool	19	845,779	44,515	45,276	98%	2
Chelsea	19	788,680	41,509	41,841	99%	3
Arsenal	19	1,140,755	60,040	60,355	99%	4
Everton	19	677,737	35,670	40,216	89%	5
Aston Villa	19	756,422	39,812	42,640	93%	6
Fulham	19	462,551	24,345	25,678	95%	7
Tottenham Hotspur	19	682,643	35,929	36,257	99%	8
West Ham	19	639,813	33,674	35,300	95%	9
Manchester City	19	814,918	42,890	47,715	90%	10
Wigan	19	349,266	18,382	25,135	73%	11
Stoke City	19	512,150	26,955	27,500	98%	12
Bolton	19	431,698	22,721	28,101	81%	13
Portsmouth	19	376,126	19,796	20,839	95%	14
Blackburn	19	446,146	23,481	31,154	75%	15
Sunderland	19	763,198	40,168	49,000	82%	16
Hull City	19	471,507	24,816	25,417	98%	17
Newcastle	19	930,642	48,981	52,387	93%	18
Middlesbrough	19	540,379	28,441	35,049	81%	19
West Bromwich Albion	19	490,726	25,828	27,901	93%	20
Overall	380	13,552,002	35,663	38,697	92%	

League match in that season. Average attendance figures varied by club and were in part dependent on the ground capacity of each club. For example, Manchester United had the highest capacity and also the highest average attendance for their home games, whereas Wigan had the lowest capacity and the lowest average attendance at home. Attendances were also influenced by the relative quality of the home team, which is demonstrated by the moderately high negative correlation ($r = -0.6$) between a club's final position in the league table and average home attendance. In other words, clubs that finish higher up in the table tend to be those that attract larger crowds at their home games.

The overall utilisation rate of 92 per cent across all matches played in the Premier League in 2008–9 is a considerable testament to the Premier League's domestic appeal. This is highlighted even further when we consider that 14 of the 20 clubs filled at least 90 per cent of available seats and no club achieved a stadium utilisation rate of less than 73 per cent. Albeit significant in their own right, match–day attendance figures are only a small component of the Premier League's domestic audience. This is because there is a limit to the number of people that each club ground can accommodate. The maximum potential live match–day attendance for all 380 Premier League fixtures in the 2008–9 season was 14.7 million. By comparison, there were 2,100 televised broadcasts of Premier League matches in the UK in 2008–9, which had a domestic cumulative audience of 583 million. Thus, for each person attending a Premier League fixture there were 40 people who watched the game live on television. Such figures serve to demonstrate the domestic importance attached to watching the Premier League in the UK. General public interest in the Premier League can be further appreciated by citing the findings from a recent survey (EPL 2010), according to which 59 per cent of the UK population aged 16–59 are either 'very interested' or 'interested' in football and of those 86 per cent (51 per cent of all respondents) are 'very interested'/'interested' in the Premier League. With every second person in the UK expressing an interest in the Premier League its popularity at home cannot be overstated.

UK television deals

Until the 1990s the broadcasting of football in particular, and sport generally, remained a buyer's market in Britain. It was when BSkyB, a pay-service satellite broadcaster, entered the scene, most notably with its bid for football's (then newly formed) Premier League matches for the 1992–97 period that the landscape of sports broadcasting in Britain changed dramatically. BSkyB, with its owners Rupert Murdoch's News Corporation (owners of Fox) used to the much stronger competition for sports broadcasting rights in the USA, simply raised the price for the rights from its artificially depressed level. There was a 250 per cent increase in the level of fees for televised football in 1992 when BSkyB won the rights for 60 live matches of the Premier League at an average cost of £38 million per year. When the deal was renegotiated in 1997 there was a further 337 per cent rise in the annual rights (MMC 1999).

The 2001–4 deal of £1.1 billion was again with BSkyB, as was the 2004–7 deal. Both these deals involved more live matches per season. The fact that there was no increase in the price BSkyB paid for the 2004–7 rights was seen by many as an indicator that the boom time for broadcasting rights was over. By 2004, for many English Premier League clubs, broadcasting income was already the single most important source of income. For Chelsea, for instance in 2003–4, 39 per cent of total revenue (£143.7 million) came from the sale of broadcasting rights compared to 37 per cent from match-day income, and 24 per cent from commercial income. Manchester United, with by far the largest capacity stadium in the Premier League (at 67,500), had the same proportion of revenue (36 per cent) for both broadcasting and match-day income. Arsenal, on the other hand, with a stadium capacity of only 38,500 had 52 per cent of its total revenue coming from broadcasting income in 2003–4, with only 29 per cent coming from match-day income (Deloitte 2005).

During the life of the 2004–7 contract, the European Commission intervened on the grounds that BSkyB was in a monopoly position in relation to the control of broadcasting rights for live Premier League games. It insisted that when the rights for the 2007–10 period were auctioned that at least one of the packages offered went to a different broadcaster. As a consequence, of the six packages offered by the Premier League for the 2007–10 period, BSkyB only secured four of them consisting of a total of 92 live matches. BSkyB paid £1.3 billion for these games at a cost of £4.76 million per game compared with an average cost over the 2004–7 period of £2.47 million

TABLE 6.6 Premier League domestic TV rights – 1992 to present

	Initial year of contract					
	1992	1997	2001	2004	2007	2010
Length of contract (years)	5	4	3	3	3	3
Broadcaster	BSkyB	BSkyB	BSkyB	BSkyB	BSkyB / Setanta / ESPN	BSkyB / ESPN
Contract value (£m)	191.5	670	1,100	1,024	1,702	1,782
Annual rights fee (£m)	38.3	167.5	366.7	341.3	567.3	594.0
Live matches per season	60	60	106	138	138	138
Fees per live match	0.6	2.8	3.5	2.5	4.1	4.3

per game, a 93 per cent increase in the cost to BSkyB. The other two packages went to an Irish television station, Setanta. Their packages consisted of 46 live games per year at a total cost of £392 million, or £2.8 million per game, considerably less than the cost to BSkyB but more than BSkyB paid for each game over the 2004–7 period. The total income to the Premier League from the new deal was £1.7 billion over three years, a massive 67 per cent increase compared to 2004–7.

In mid-2009 Setanta ceased trading in Britain after it was unable to meet a payment deadline to the Premier League amongst a number of sporting organisations and its allocation of matches for the 2009–10 season was subsequently sold to the Disney-owned ESPN. The latest domestic television rights deal covering the period 2010–13 has yet again increased in value to £1.8 billion for a total of 414 live matches (138 per year), of which BSkyB and ESPN have secured 345 (115 per year) and 69 (23 per year) games respectively. The intervention by the European Commission resulted in a considerable escalation in the price of domestic broadcasting rights. Moreover, this phenomenon is also being mirrored outside the UK.

International consumption

In recent years, there has been a growth in the value for broadcasting rights of the Premier League in overseas markets. In 2001, the Premier League made £1.1 billion from the sale of domestic TV rights and £178 million from overseas rights. For the 2007–2010 contract, the domestic rights cost £1.7 billion and the foreign rights had leapt to £625 million, claimed to be the biggest overseas deal for sport in the world at that time (Bevan and Stevenson 2008). Broadcaster NowTV paid around £100 million to secure the rights for Hong Kong alone. Showtime Arabia stumped up around £60 million for the Middle East and North African market and WinTV spent £50 million to show games in China. The overseas rights are due for renegotiation in 2010 for the next three years when the cost of overseas rights is expected to match, if not exceed, the domestic price tag of £1.8 billion. The rationale for this rapid growth is the ever-increasing popularity of Premier League beyond UK

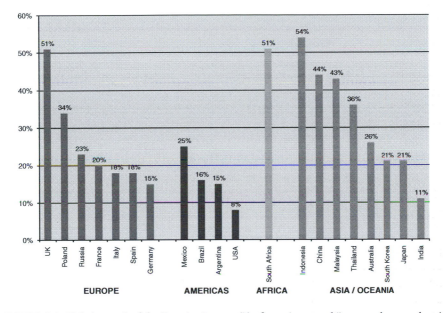

FIGURE 6.4 Global appeal of the Premier League (% of very interested/interested respondents)
Source: EPL Global Fan Survey

shores, particularly in Asia. By 2004, the Premier League was the most watched sport in Malaysia, Thailand and Singapore. In 2005, it was the most watched televised football league in China, rising from third position two years ago. Gratton and Solberg (2007: 170) report that, according to an internet survey, 83 per cent of Chinese football fans preferred watching the English Premier League to matches in the China Super League (CSL). A more recent survey provides an indication of the global appeal of the Premier League (EPL 2010). Figure 6.4 shows the percentage of respondents from countries in which the survey was undertaken who stated that they were 'very interested' or 'interested' in the Premier League. Notably, the level of interest in Indonesia (54 per cent) is higher than in the UK (51 per cent) and the interest in South Africa is equivalent to the UK.

The international pull of the Premier League is reflected in the worldwide coverage afforded to it and number of people who watch Premier League games abroad. Live matches are screened in more than 200 countries across Europe, Asia, Oceania, Africa, the Americas and the Middle East. A variety of kick-off times enable fans in all continents to watch matches at convenient times. An estimated 1 billion people watched the Premier League game between Arsenal and Manchester United in November 2007 boosted by it being shown during the evening across the Far East (Wilson 2007). Following a football club is almost as easy in Thailand or Hong Kong as it is in England – and that is why clubs are increasingly turning to the overseas market in order to boost their fan base and their revenue streams. A Liverpool fan in Thailand, for example, would be able to watch Steven Gerrard and colleagues in action at 3 o'clock (English time) on a Saturday, whereas a UK-based fan would not unless he or

TABLE 6.7 Broadcast and viewing figures for the 2008–9 Premier League

Continent	No. of broadcasts	% of broadcast	Cumulative audience (mn)	% of audience
Europe (ex. UK)	25,200	36	556.5	21
Asia	24,500	35	927.5	35
Africa	7,000	10	159.0	6
Middle East	4,200	6	79.5	3
Oceania	2,800	4	53.0	2
North America and Caribbean	2,800	4	53.0	2
South and Central America	1,400	2	238.5	9
Overseas sub-total	67,900	97	2067.0	78
UK	2,100	3	583.0	22
Total	70,000	100	2650.0	100

she was attending the game due to the nature of the rights package (Bevan and Stevenson 2008).

In the 2008–9 season, there were 70,000 broadcasts of Premier League games, of which 67,900 (97 per cent) were screened outside the UK – see Table 6.7. Over 500 million homes received approximately 100,000 hours of coverage, providing an estimated cumulative global television audience of 2.65 billion viewers. This equates to an average audience of around 70 million per week based on 38 match weeks. The number of overseas viewers (2.07 billion) outnumbers the domestic UK audience (583 million) by a ratio of 3.5:1.

In recent years, the popularity of the Premier League abroad has soared even as clubs spend their pre-seasons travelling across the world to take their product to those countries which have a huge appetite for English football. Starting in 2003, Premier League affiliated pre-season tournaments have been held in Asia which in addition to English clubs have featured the Malaysia and Thailand national teams. Three of the Premier League's so-called 'big four' clubs – Manchester United, Chelsea and Liverpool – have between them been to the USA, South Africa, Hong Kong, China, Japan and South Korea; only Arsenal have stayed in Europe. Many clubs have also signed players from these countries – Manchester United obtained South Korea's Ji-Sung Park in 2005, Everton bought China's Li Tie in 2003, and Manchester City took three Thai players on trial in 2007 (Bevan and Stevenson 2008).

Gratton and Solberg (2007) note that viewers of TV sports programmes in general have preferences for watching competitors and clubs from their own countries. The fact that the English Premier League has recruited a large number of foreign players, from Europe and elsewhere, has stimulated interest in the Premier League in external markets. In 1992 there were just 11 non-British or Irish footballers in the Premier League, but by 2007 this had increased to over 250. Over the years, overseas players have helped shape and develop the British game (EPL 2011). In the 2009–10

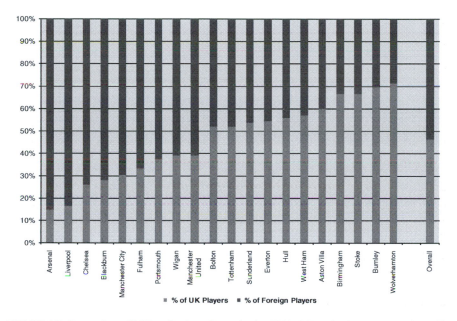

FIGURE 6.5 Proportion of UK to foreign players in the 2008–9 Premier League

season, it is estimated that the number of foreign-born players representing Premier League clubs had increased to the point that non-UK players outnumbered domestic players. Foreign nationals now account for 53.5 per cent of all current Premier League squads. The corresponding figure for the same teams in the 1989–90 season (of the then First Division) was only 8.4 per cent. Now, Premier League teams have on average 13 foreign-born players within their ranks, up from an average of two per team around 20 years ago (Williams 2009). A total of 66 countries are represented in the Premier League. A breakdown of player nationalities by continent is as follows: Europe 33 (including the UK home nations and the Republic of Ireland); Africa 14; the Americas 13; Asia 4; and, Australia/Oceania 2 (EPL 2010). Two decades ago, the teams making up the 2008–9 Premier League could only boast 12 players born outside the Commonwealth between them. More than half of the current Premier League's clubs could field an entire starting line-up of foreign-born players (Williams 2009). Indeed there have even been matches where one of the clubs only had foreign players.

In some cases, clubs have been accused of taking into account commercial concerns, particularly in relation to recruiting talent from Asia, rather than emphasising the player's skills. The following story of how Everton Football Club became the biggest football team in China in a few short months in 2002–3 is an interesting story of sport in the global marketplace:

> In July 2002, Everton became the first European football club to sign a sponsorship deal with a Chinese company. The deal with Keijan, China's top mobile phone manufacturer, was for two years and was reported to be worth £1 million per season. As part of the deal two Chinese internationals, Lie Tie and Li Weifeng

were to come to Everton on 12-month loans. Everton also planned to tour China, set up a Chinese based club, and create a Mandarin page on its official website through which it could sell merchandise.

(Gratton and Solberg 2007)

Keijan, in reverse, saw the deal as a way of extending its brand into Europe. Also by televising Everton's games live in China it gave the company an opportunity to raise its profile, where it faced stiff competition from European and Japanese brands. By the time the 2002–3 season began in August 2002, Everton had overtaken Liverpool and Manchester United as China's favourite team. During the early part of the season, one of the Chinese players Lie Tie established a regular place in Everton's first team line-up, something many did not expect at the beginning of the season, and Everton enjoyed their best ever start to a Premiership season. On 1 January 2003, 365 million Chinese viewers watched Everton play Manchester City live on Chinese television. As well as Lie Tie in the Everton line-up, Manchester City also had their Chinese star Sun Jihai playing. The result was a television audience in the Far East 200 times larger than the same game would have attracted in England. By February 2003, the Chinese version of Everton's website had received more than 3 million hits since it was set up in August 2002.

Although the Keijan sponsorship deal was not renewed after the two years, Plowright (2008) gives an example of how Everton in 2008 was still using Chinese television to target the Chinese market:

> Everton partnered with Chinese regional TV station Hunan TV to produce a reality TV series, Soccer Prince, in which thousands of young Chinese football hopefuls from across the country battled it out to win a place at Everton's famous youth training academy, a centre that has produced talent such as England and Manchester United star Wayne Rooney. Everton's brand name was a prominent feature throughout the series, which attracted an estimated 130 million viewers, and the winner, 19-year old Jin Hui, arrived at the Merseyside in May to train with his new colleagues.
>
> Plowright (2008)

Conclusions

The most important factors that have driven the globalisation of the sport market over the last two decades have been the developments in the sports broadcasting market that have been discussed in this chapter. The explosion in the price of the broadcasting rights to major sports events has been the basis of the increasing power of GSOs that we discussed in Chapter 3, even though this has been controlled to some extent in some countries by listed events legislation which prevents open competition for these rights by insisting that some of these events are shown on free-to-air channels. Partly because of these restrictions, these events are broadcast to a huge global audience so that global sports corporations use the event to showcase their products through advertising, sponsorship and athlete endorsements connected to the events. Global non-sport corporations use sponsorship of the events to reinforce their global market position again because no other sponsorship vehicle can attract such large global television audiences. At the domestic level, new distribution methods and broadcasting platforms, including satellite and cable, have increased the competition in the market for domestic sports rights. New broadcasters, such as BSkyB in the UK, have transformed the television landscape for sport and the major reason for BSkyB's success has been its ownership of sports rights, most notably for the English Premier League. More recently, the EPL has obtained massive fees for the international distribution rights with games now broadcast live in over 200 countries throughout the world. An English domestic football competition has become a global product. All these changes have happened in a remarkably small period of time. There are signs that this pace of change is now slowing as the global sport market starts to mature. This is because most of the world already has access to the major sports events, the broadcasting of which has driven the globalisation process. The doubling and trebling of broadcasting rights for major sports events that we have seen since the early 1990s is unlikely to happen again. Broadcasting rights for these events are also unlikely to decrease. Instead, they should remain fairly stable with further increases on a much smaller level than previously.

7

SPORT SPONSORSHIP

Introduction

The previous chapter has demonstrated the escalating financial reliance of sport generally and major sports events in particular on revenues from broadcasting. With the demand for watching sport and broadcasting of sporting events at an all-time high, innumerable opportunities exist for companies to 'buy into' the broadcast of sport-related programming in order to be able to showcase themselves to a mass audience during and around that programme. This type of association can be termed broadcast and media sponsorship of sport (Schwartz and Hunter 2008) and the cost of purchasing such exposure can be very expensive depending on the profile of the sports concerned. By way of example, in the UK exotic juice drink brand Rubicon have reportedly spent up to £5 million in 2010 to sponsor a Summer of Cricket on Sky Sports, opening with the channel's broadcast coverage of the ICC Twenty 20 World Cup in the West Indies (Talking Retail 2010).

The demand for broadcasting of major sports events is not spread evenly across all sports or indeed all competitions. For example, the global demand for watching televised football is likely to be more than, say, swimming and similarly the FIFA World Cup can be expected to attract higher broadcast revenues than events of equivalent status in many other sports. As a result, there can be a considerable variation in the broadcast revenue generating capability of different sports and also between different competitions within the same sports. Even for the largest and most popular sports events such as the Olympic Games or the FIFA World Cup, economic viability usually depends on the ability of the event organisers to raise substantial revenue through sponsorship. Notwithstanding this comment, the level of sponsorship is often linked to how much coverage an event will achieve in national and international markets. The greater the amount of broadcast coverage afforded to an event, the higher the number of opportunities is for the event sponsors to be visible to target audiences, which in turn raises the cost (price) of the association between the sponsor and the event. This chapter plots the growth of sponsorship in sport overall in recent years and examines the emerging trends within the different types of sports sponsorship using examples from across the globe.

The growth of sport sponsorship

After income from the sale of broadcasting rights, sponsorship income is now the second most important source of income to the global sport market. In this section, we examine how the value of sponsorship and sponsorship spending on sport has grown based on a scrutiny of figures quoted by different sources at different points in time. According to Smart (2005), the global sponsorship market was estimated to be worth $10 billion in 1993, which grew to $27 billion in 2003; and in 2003, more than two-thirds of that market, $18 billion, was attributable to sport-related business activity. In Britain alone, the sports sponsorship industry was valued at around £1 billion by 1999 (including contract fees, exploitation and other ancillary expenditure), despite hardly existing as an economic activity before 1970, and by 2002 the market was estimated to have a total value of £1.5 billion (Gratton and Taylor 2000). More recent figures available from International Events Group (IEG 2009) indicate that the global sponsorship market was worth $44 billion in 2009, up from $43 billion in 2008. Moreover, in 2008, according to IEG, sport accounted for around 68 per cent (or $11.3 billion) of the total sponsorship pie in the United States and Canada of $16.6 billion, which was seven times more than the next largest sector, 'entertainment tours and attractions' ($1.6 billion) – see Table 7.1. If we accept that the share of sport within the global sponsorship market is commensurate with the

TABLE 7.1 North American sponsorship spending

Sector	2006		2007		2008		2009		2010 (projected)	
	($bn)	%	($bn)	%	($bn)	%	($bn)	%	($bn)	%
Sports	8.94	66.8	9.94	66.7	11.40	68.6	11.28	68.4	11.60	67.9
Arts	0.74	5.6	0.81	5.4	0.83	5.0	0.82	5.0	0.84	4.9
Entertainment tours and attractions	1.38	10.3	1.56	10.5	1.63	9.8	1.64	9.9	1.74	10.2
Festivals, fairs, annual events	0.61	4.6	0.70	4.7	0.75	4.5	0.76	4.6	0.78	4.6
Cause	1.30	9.7	1.44	9.7	1.52	9.2	1.51	9.2	1.61	9.4
Associations and Membership organisations	0.40	3.0	0.46	3.1	0.48	2.9	0.50	3.0	0.51	3.0
Totals	13.37	100.0	14.91	100.0	16.61	100.0	16.51	100.0	17.08	100.0

Source: Compiled from IEG Sponsorship Report (2009)

amount of money spent by companies in North America, then the value of sports-related sponsorship in 2008 would have been almost $30 billion. However, there is alternative evidence that this may in fact be an underestimate of the value of the worldwide spending on sports sponsorship in that year.

Many sponsorship deals will never be revealed in statistics because they are at local and regional levels and involve sponsorship arrangements between relatively small firms and small local sports organisations. Furthermore, often a large proportion of time and resources of the promotion and marketing departments of companies is taken up with sponsorship arrangements i.e. printing, publicity, and entertainment which fall outside the initial sponsorship fee (Gratton and Taylor 2000). The World Sponsorship Monitor (TWSM) analyses sponsorship deals reported in the international media with a value of $75,000 or more. TWSM's 2008 Annual Review confirms that sport continues to dominate the global sponsorship market but accounts for 79 per cent of all sponsorship deals and 88 per cent of total value. The total number of sponsorships reported in 2008 was 1,333, which despite the prevailing economic climate at the time, compares favourably against corresponding figure of 1,196 in 2007. William Fenton, editor of TWSM, points out that:

> in 2008 the proportion of higher value sponsorships (valued at over $10 million) over the total sample was actually higher (19 per cent in 2008 compared to 13 per cent in 2007). This is because brands are seeking out partnerships with the mega events, such as the Olympics, American football's NFL, Formula One and major football brands, which draw huge television audiences. This was borne out in 2008 by the number of sponsorships announced for the Beijing Olympics as well as the London Games in 2012.
>
> (Sport Business 2010b)

Using TWSM figures as a proxy, the value of global sports sponsorship in 2008 would have been as high as $38 billion. The latest figures from TWSM available at the time of writing show that in the first quarter of 2009, compared to the same period the previous year, a similar number of new deals were signed overall (300 compared to 302). It is worth noting that the number of withdrawals by brands from sponsorship increased from 24 in 2008 to 42 in 2009. Although it is not known how many renewals were affected across the whole year in 2009, given that many deals are signed over three or more years it is likely that these would not be affected by the global recession. However, in early 2009, TWSM was predicting an increase in lower-value deals of a shorter duration and that the properties in between the premium events and the more common lower-value properties will be squeezed hard.

Reasons for sports sponsorship growth

There are a number of reasons why the sponsorship of sport has grown so rapidly. One of these is the increase in the media attention given to sport, as illustrated by the amount of coverage afforded to events such as the Olympic Games and FIFA World

Cup (see Chapter 6). Another reason cited by Schwartz and Hunter (2008) is the desire for companies to target consumers through the sports lifestyle through non-advertising efforts. Yet another reason for the growth of sponsorship spending on sport may be attributed to the fact that, in contrast to other industries, there is considerable interest in sport from non-sports corporations. For example, in 2005, Nike was the only company from the sports industry that was in the top 10 corporations engaged in sports sponsorship, with most sponsorship coming from the food and beverage industry and the automotive industry (Schwartz and Hunter 2008).

TWSM's 2008 Annual Review revealed that since 2005 the automotive industry has been the most prolific spender on sports sponsorship, signing 143 deals in 2008, up from 125 in 2007, followed by the banking sector with 110 deals (127 in 2007). Although sports clothing remains a major sponsoring industry it is only the third biggest, signing 97 deals in 2008 compared to 68 the previous year. Tele-communications continues to be important as fifth-biggest industry in terms of number of deals signed (72 in 2008 compared to 53 in 2007). BT, Nortel, and Deutsche Telekom were the third, fourth, and tenth biggest spending sponsors. For the first time, the travel industry is in the top 10 sponsoring industries, following a number of deals between sports clubs and travel destinations or tourist boards. In total, there were 37 deals signed by the travel sector in 2008, up from 13 the previous year. The number of airline deals also increased to 59, from 46.

It is worth noting that although non-sports companies are more prominent in terms of the aggregate volume of their sports sponsorship expenditure, six of the top ten most valuable deals in 2008 were signed by clothing and kit makers – Nike and Adidas. The two biggest deals of 2008 were signed by Nike. The first was with the French Football Federation starting in 2011, covering seven years and worth $474.6 million. The second was with Italian Serie A club, Inter Milan, worth $206 million over 10 years.

Perhaps unsurprisingly, the most sponsored sport is football both in terms of the total number and the total value of reported deals. In 2008, there were 262 football sponsorship deals compared to 218 in the previous year. Five of the top 10 deals signed in 2008 were for football, together totalling over $1 billion alone – see Table 7.2. Tennis became a more sought after property for sponsors, moving into the top 10 in terms of number of deals signed. The sixth biggest deal of 2008 was Nike's $118-million sponsorship agreement with Swiss tennis superstar Roger Federer. Motorsport fell out from the top 10 most sponsored sports in 2008. Formula 1 experienced fewer major headline deals in 2007, though notable exceptions were the Olympus $30 million deal with the McLaren team and Reebok's $20 million deal with 2008 Formula 1 Champion Lewis Hamilton.

The IEG Sponsorship Report projects a 4.5 per cent growth in worldwide sponsorship spending for 2010 to $46 billion. According to them, the largest gains will come from Africa and South America, in part due to activity and interest surrounding South Africa's hosting the 2010 FIFA World Cup and a developing sponsorship marketplace in countries such as Brazil, which will host both the 2014 World Cup and 2016 Olympic Games. So, it is likely that the value of sport within the overall sponsorship market is likely to increase even further.

TABLE 7.2 Top 20 sponsorship deals in 2008

Rank	Sponsor	Sponsorship	Value ($m)	Duration (Years)	Annual value ($m)
1	Nike	French Football Federation (from 2011)	475	7	68
2	Nike	Internazionale	206	10	21
3	BT	London Olympics 2012 Tier One sponsor	160	5	32
4	Nortel	London Olympics 2012 Tier One sponsor	150	4	38
5	Adidas	AC Milan	123	10	12
6	Nike	Roger Federer	118	10	12
7	Adidas	Ajax	110	10	11
8	Adidas	Russian Football Union	100	8	13
9	BP	London Olympics 2012 Tier One sponsor	100	4	25
10	British Airways	London Olympics 2012 Tier One sponsor	98	5	20
11	Adidas	All Blacks	90	10	9
12	Consol Energy	Pittsburgh Penguins NHL stadium	84	21	4
13	Dekra	Deutscher Fußball-Bund (DFB)	80	4	20
14	Deutsche Telekom	Deutscher Fußball-Bund (DFB)	80	4	20
15	Miller	Dallas Cowboys	80	10	8
16	Rogers Communications	Buffalo Bills	77	5	15
17	Automobile Club of South Carolina	Auto Speedway of Southern California	75	10	8
18	Banco Itau	Brazilian Football Confederation	75	5	15
19	Budweiser	NHL sponsorship through Bud lite	75	3	25
20	Olympus	US Open and US Open Series Official Camera	70	6	12

Howard and Crompton (2004) identify nine major factors in the external environment that have collectively stimulated sports sponsorship growth, summarised as follows: (i) the advertising clutter resulting from a proliferation of television channels caused companies to seek an alternative communication medium; (ii) the cost of television advertising escalated while the audience fragmented; (iii) the increased number of channels created a need for more programming and sport is relatively inexpensive to produce; (iv) tobacco and liquor companies were banned from television advertising; (v) commercialisation of sport has been increasingly accepted by organising bodies; (vi) sponsorships associated with the 1984 Los Angeles Olympic Games enjoyed high profile success; (vii) market segmentation has emerged as a guiding marketing principle; (viii) the need to enhance relations with distributors developed because fewer but larger companies exercise increasingly more control in distribution channels; and, (ix) the increasing tendency of public agencies to charge for additional costs they incur as a result of an increase in the sports organisation's costs of staging an event.

In addition to the external environmental changes that have facilitated growth in sponsorship, there has been increasing recognition of unique qualities that give it intrinsic merit. Sponsorship offers a fifth communication vehicle that complements personal selling, advertising, publicity and incentives, rather than supplanting any of them. Sponsorship has two special strengths. First, it contributes to establishing a position in consumers' minds that differentiates one product from another, through its role in image enhancement. Second, it facilitates opportunities for a company to establish a more intimate relationship with its target audience than is feasible with the other communication vehicles (Howard and Crompton 2004).

Areas of sport sponsorship

Schwartz and Hunter (2008) have identified six broad categories of sports sponsorship and they discuss each of these distinct areas mainly in the context of the sports sponsorship industry in the United States. The six categories include: sports governing body sponsorship; sports team sponsorship; athlete sponsorship; broadcast and media sponsorship; sports facility sponsorship; and, sports event sponsorship. They note that the six categories collectively accounted for the majority of the multi-billion dollar sports sponsorship industry in the United States in 2005. The classification presented by Schwartz and Hunter is a useful way in which to micro-analyse the sports sponsorship industry and explore emerging trends within the different market segments. As demonstrated by Table 7.2, governing body and major event sponsorship tend to dominate the higher value deals. Naming rights deals are relatively rare – accounting for just 4 per cent of all sponsorship deals signed – but they attract proportionally higher rights fees (Sport Business 2010b). In 2008, 7 per cent of total committed investment went into naming rights. Naming rights boomed in 2006 and 2007 with notable deals such as Barclays' record breaking $400 million naming deal for the new arena of the NBA basketball team New Jersey Nets. The biggest naming rights deal in terms of total investment was signed by the Consol Energy company, which committed $84 million over 21 years to be the naming rights sponsor of the stadium of the NHL ice-hockey team the Pittsburgh Penguins (the twelfth-biggest of all sponsorship deals signed in 2008). In terms of annual committed fee, the two biggest venue deals are those signed by drinks company Anheuser-Busch and financial services firm MetLife for the new Meadowlands Stadium – the new home of the NFL teams, the New York Jets and New York Giants. Under their deals, the two companies will pay a reported $8 million per year each over five years. Outside the USA, the biggest naming rights deal was in Germany where Mercedes named Bundesliga club Stuttgart's 55,000 seat stadium the Mercedes-Benz Arena, in a deal worth $31 million over 30 years. Also in Germany the Signal Iduna Group signed an early five-year extension to its contract with Borussia Dortmund to retain its sponsorship of the 'Signal Iduna Park', Germany's biggest football stadium (Sport Business 2010b).

The corporations that tend to enter into sponsorship with governing bodies tend to be larger, national, or multinational companies, mainly due to the large financial investment required with these sponsorships (Schwartz and Hunter 2008). Perhaps the most widely known governing bodies of sport globally are FIFA and the IOC, who control the rights to the two largest sporting events on the planet, the Football World Cup and the Olympic Games respectively. With this in mind, it is worth examining the sponsorship arrangements of these truly iconic organisations.

FIFA and the Football World Cup

FIFA was the first global sports organisation for which corporate sponsorship became a major source of revenue generation, with the World Cup becoming the main tournament for securing lucrative global commercial sponsorship agreements and for auctioning the sale of global television broadcasting rights (Smart 2005). Following the election of João Havelange as president in 1974, FIFA's future development was considered to be bound up with the deployment of appropriate marketing strategies targeted at potential global corporate sponsors. In his campaign for the FIFA presidency, Havelange had promised to increase the number of countries participating in the World Cup Finals, to introduce a World Youth tournament, and to enhance the global appeal of football by establishing a programme to help develop the game in Africa and Asia. Such commitments necessitated significant increases in funding. With the assistance of Horst Dassler and Patrick Nally, who from 1977 to 1982 shared the sports marketing partnership SMPI (Société Monégasque de Promotion Internationale), FIFA and President Havelange set out to establish exclusive marketing rights agreements with major global corporations. They began with the 1978 World Cup tournament in Argentina, for which contracts were negotiated with six major corporate sponsors, including Coca-Cola, Gillette and Seiko (Sugden and Tomlinson 1998; Smit 2006). This established a template that would be followed in subsequent tournaments (Table 7.3).

The 1982 World Cup tournament in Spain was the first to have an organised corporate sponsorship programme, with a reported $19 million being raised in total from nine 'partner' sponsors. For the 2006 tournament in Germany, the 15 partner companies paid on average $35 million each to be a part of the FIFA sponsorship programme (Maidment 2006). From 2007, FIFA's global commercial strategy became even more exclusive as prospective marketing partners were grouped into three categories; 'six FIFA Partners, six to eight FIFA World Cup sponsors and four to six National Supporters'. Appropriately the first to sign up as a FIFA Partner for the period 2007–14 was Adidas, which paid $350 million, followed by Hyundai, sum undisclosed, Sony $305 million, Coca-Cola $500 million (up to 2020), and Emirates Airline $195 million (Viscusi 2006).

At present, the FIFA Sponsorship Programme covers the period from 2007–14, including the flagship FIFA World Cups in 2010 and 2014, and now classifies prospective marketing partners into three categories: FIFA Partner, FIFA World Cup

TABLE 7.3 Official Partners of the FIFA World Cup 1982–2010

	2010	2006	2002	1998	1994	1990	1986	1982
Adidas	x	x	x	x				
Coca-Cola	x	x	x	x	x	x	x	x
Emirates	x	x						
Hyundai-Kia Motors (2002–2006: Hyundai)	x	x	x					
Sony	x							
Visa	x							
Alfa Romeo						x		
Anheuser-Busch		x	x	x		x	x	
Avaya		x	x					
Bata							x	
Canon				x	x	x	x	x
Cinzano							x	
Continental		x						
Deutsche Telekom		x						
Energizer					x			
Fuji Xerox			x					
Fujifilm		x	x	x	x	x	x	x
Gillette		x	x	x	x	x	x	x
Iveco								x
JVC			x	x	x	x	x	x
Korea Telekom/NTT			x					
MasterCard		x	x	x	x			
McDonald's		x	x	x	x			
Metaxa								x
Opel (1994: General Motors)				x	x		x	
Phillips		x	x	x	x	x	x	
R.J. Reynolds (1986: Camel/1982: Winston)							x	x
Seiko							x	x
Snickers (1990: Mars /m&m's)				x	x	x		
Toshiba		x	x					
Vini di Italia						x		
Yahoo!		x	x					
Total number	6	15	15	12	11	10	12	9

Sponsor, and National Supporter. A FIFA Partner enjoys the highest level of association with FIFA. In short, this means they own rights to a broader range of FIFA
activities – be they competitions, special events or development programmes – as
well as exclusive marketing assets. A FIFA World Cup Sponsor's rights are limited to
the FIFA World Cup on a global basis. They consist of the right to category exclusivity, brand association, select marketing assets and secondary media exposure. The
National Supporter is a category of association which allows local companies to

promote an association with the FIFA World Cup within the host country. The rights include category exclusivity, association, local marketing programmes and domestic media exposure (FIFA 2007).

IOC and the Olympic Games

Olympic sponsorship is an agreement between an Olympic organisation and a corporation, whereby the corporation is granted the rights to specific Olympic intellectual property and Olympic marketing opportunities in exchange for financial support and goods and services contributions. Olympic sponsorship programmes operate on the principle of product-category exclusivity. Under the direction of the IOC, the Olympic Family works to preserve the value of Olympic properties and to protect the exclusive rights of Olympic sponsors (IOC 2008).

At the 1976 Olympic Games, there were 628 sponsors and suppliers but only US $7 million in revenue was generated. For the 1984 Games sponsorship was organised into three categories: 'Official Sponsor' (34), companies with 'supplier' rights (64) and 'licences' (65). The IOC describes the 1984 Games as inaugurating the most successful era of corporate sponsorship in Olympic history. In 1985, International Sport and Leisure (ISL), the most influential sports marketing agency throughout the 1980s and 1990s, drew on experience gained with FIFA when assisting the IOC to establish a lucrative marketing rights plan, the Olympic Partner (TOP) programme (Smit 2006; Sugden and Tomlinson 1998). The programme offers exclusive global marketing rights to a select group of corporate sponsors who pay a higher premium in exchange for the greater value flowing from an exclusive relationship with one of the world's leading sporting events. The attractiveness of the TOP programme to global corporations can be gauged from the fact that, as the IOC reports, 'the program enjoys one of the highest sponsorship renewal rates of any sports property'. Over the 25-year period that the programme has been in existence, the revenue generated from sponsorship agreements with a limited number of global corporate partners has grown significantly (Table 7.4).

The Olympic Partners (TOP) programme is the worldwide sponsorship programme managed by the IOC. The IOC created the TOP programme in 1985 in order to develop a diversified revenue base for the Olympic Games and to establish long-term

TABLE 7.4 TOP programme evolution

Quadrennium	Games	Partners	NOCs	Revenue
1985–1988	Calgary/Seoul	9	159	US$96 million
1989–1992	Albertville/Barcelona	12	169	US$172 million
1993–1996	Lillehammer/Atlanta	10	197	US$279 million
1997–2000	Nagano/Sydney	11	199	US$579 million
2001–2004	Salt Lake City/Athens	11	202	US$663 million
2005–2008	Turin/Beijing	12	205	US$866 million

corporate partnerships that would benefit the Olympic Movement as a whole. The TOP programme operates on a four-year term in line with the Olympic quad-rennium. The TOP programme generates support for the Organising Committees of the Olympic Games and Olympic Winter Games, the NOCs, and the IOC. The TOP programme provides each worldwide Olympic partner with exclusive global marketing rights and opportunities within a designated product or service category. The global marketing rights include partnerships with the IOC, all active NOCs and their Olympic teams, and the two OCOGs and the Games of each quadrennium. The TOP Partners may exercise these rights worldwide and may activate marketing initiatives with all the members of the Olympic Movement that participate in the TOP programme (IOC 2008).

The Olympic Games domestic sponsorship programme is managed by the OCOG within the host country under the direction of the IOC. The programmes support the operations of the OCOG, the planning and staging of the Games, the host country NOC, and the host country Olympic team. The Olympic Games domestic sponsorship programme grants marketing rights within the host country or territory only. The host country NOC and the host country Olympic team participate in the OCOG sponsorship programme because the Marketing Plan Agreement requires the OCOG and the host country NOC to centralise and coordinate all marketing initiatives within the host country (IOC 2008).

Table 7.5 and 7.6 provide an overview of the history of the OCOG sponsorship programmes at the Summer and Winter Olympic Games respectively.

Why do corporations sponsor sport?

To understand why firms sponsor sport, one starting point is to look at the economics of advertising. The initial analysis of the advertising decision assumes the firm to have the overall objective of profit maximisation. Advertising aims to move the demand

TABLE 7.5 Olympic Games: history of OCOG sponsorship programmes

Olympic Games	Number of partners	Revenue and support
1996 Atlanta	111	US$426 million
2000 Sydney	93	US$492 million
2004 Athens	38	US$302 million
2008 Beijing	51	US$1,218 million

TABLE 7.6 Olympic Winter Games: history of OCOG sponsorship programmes

Olympic Winter Games	Number of partners	Revenue and support
1998 Nagano	26	US$163 million
2002 Salt Lake City	53	US$494 million
2006 Turin	57	US$348 million

curve of the product to the right, although at the same time the costs of advertising will raise overall costs. Advertising increases profits as long as the increased sales revenue more than matches the increased costs.

The economic research indicates that one of the greatest problems with the advertising decision of the firm is the uncertainty associated with the return from this expenditure. The risk or uncertainty associated with the advertising decision is compounded by the view of some economists that advertising should be treated as an investment, because it yields returns over a period of time. They argue that advertising is the main means by which a firm builds its name and goodwill over time. The longer the period of time over which the revenue stream is affected, the greater will be the risk and uncertainty associated with the advertising decision. Also, this view indicates that the return to advertising involves immeasurable variables such as 'name and goodwill'.

Sponsorship can be viewed as part of the profit-maximisation behaviour of a firm. In this context, the primary motive is increased sales. The risk and uncertainty of revenue response to advertising expenditure would lead firms to diversify into alternative marketing strategies, of which sponsorship is one.

All the evidence on sports sponsorship by firms indicates that this type of marketing/advertising behaviour is highly risky in terms of expected returns. Because of the riskiness of this type of marketing strategy, we should expect some involvement (since returns could conceivably be large) but not too much. This is consistent with the observed behaviour of firms keeping sponsorship activity below 5 per cent of total marketing expenditure.

The sports business management and marketing literature has adopted a broader approach than the economic one to identify benefits to the sponsoring firm. Crompton (1995) has indicated four motives of business for sponsoring sport: image enhancement, increased awareness (of product and firm), hospitality opportunities, and product trial, or sales opportunities.

Marketing expenditure aimed at building the corporate image is increasingly important, and is closely associated with the investment motive for advertising. It is also often associated with some of the industries that are closely connected to sponsorship: banks, insurance companies and oil companies. Since sport is believed to have a healthy image, the idea is to carry over the image to the company and its product. Strength, competitiveness and the will to win are part of both sport and the competitive business environment. By associating elite performers with the product, the aim is to create an elite image for the company.

Another motive for sponsorship is to change the perceived image of a company to one more favourable to the company's products in a specific market. Increased awareness of both the company and the product is particularly important for those companies with a low level of awareness or for those who are introducing a new product and wish to raise awareness of it.

Because of the multiplicity of objectives associated with sponsorship it becomes difficult to monitor whether or not sponsorship has been successful. If it were simply a matter of profit maximisation, or even sales maximisation, some testing would be possible. Even then, establishing any clear statistical links with this expenditure and sales is very difficult.

Measuring the effectiveness of sponsorship

The central concept underlying sponsorship is exchange theory, which is one of the most prominent theoretical perspectives in the social sciences. It has two main precepts: (i) two or more parties exchange resources; and (ii) the resources offered by each party must be equally valued by the reciprocating parties. In response to the first precept of exchange theory, sport organisations and businesses have multiple resources that they may use as 'currency' to facilitate an exchange. The sport facility or event may offer businesses increased awareness, image enhancement, product trial or sales opportunities. Companies in return may offer support through investments of money, media exposure or in-kind services. The second precept of exchange theory suggests that a corporate partner will ask two questions, 'What's in it for me?' and 'How much will it cost me?' The trade-off is weighed between what will be gained and what will have to be given up. A key feature of this second precept is that the exchange is perceived to be fair by both sides. The fairness issue is resolved through the use of evaluation studies that measure the benefits that a company receives from its sponsorship investment (Crompton 2004).

Despite both its obvious role in the context of validating the legitimacy of the exchange and all the lip-service given to the importance of evaluation, 40 per cent of 200 sponsoring companies with major sponsorship investments reported spending nothing on research to measure the impact of their investments, while an additional 35 per cent reported spending 1 per cent or less of their sponsorship budget on impact evaluation.

However, many of these companies expressed the belief that evaluation should be a responsibility of the sports organisation, and 68 per cent of respondents reported that such organisations did not match their expectation in this area (IEG 2002). In contrast to the widespread lack of investment in evaluation, Coca-Cola, one of the largest and most experienced sponsors of sport, allocates between 3 and 10 per cent of its rights fees for evaluation (IEG 1999).

There are two factors that make assessing the impact of sponsorship investments challenging. First, sponsorship is typically used as a platform for focussing the message of multiple other promotional tools. This makes it difficult to isolate the specific impact of a sponsorship. Even if other promotional tools are not being used simultaneously, there is likely to be some carry-over effect from previous marketing communications efforts that make isolating the impact of a specific sponsorship difficult. These challenges can be addressed by the use of statistical models. A brand's historical sales data are likely to be available, as well as information on its historical spending on advertising, sales promotion, price discounting and other factors. This enables statistical models to be constructed that isolate the effects of each element on sales (Horn and Buken 1999).

A second challenge in evaluation is to account for uncontrollable environmental factors. Changes in sales levels may be attributable to changes in the marketing environment (for example, an increase or reduction in the intensity of competitive effort, or varying levels of discretionary income as a result of changes in economic conditions) rather than the sponsorships (Meenaghan 1991).

Crompton (2004) identifies three broad techniques for evaluating the effectiveness of sponsorship, namely media exposure; changes in awareness, image, or intent to purchase; and, changes in sales. The most frequently used measure is to assess the extent and value of media coverage the product or company receives. It usually involves quantifying the duration of television coverage, including both verbal and visual mentions, the duration of radio mentions and the extent of press coverage as measured in single column inches. Typically, these media mentions are tracked and assigned a monetary value based on the paid advertising rate. For example, Joyce Julius and Associates indicated that its Mid-west university client's sponsorship package would draw $720,000 of media value over the season (Masterman 2007; Masterman and Wood 2006). Similarly, the results of an evaluation of Imperial Leather's sponsorship of the 2002 Commonwealth Games consisted of a mixture of media coverage/exposure measures (Hawtin 2004):

- Eighty-nine per cent share of television exposure on the first day of the athletics that generated six and a half hours of TV presence (logo sightings).
- Two hundred and fifty-three branded photographs in national press during athletics days.
- Exposure of the brand in the UK media equated to £889,882 of additional coverage.

Another example of the use of media equivalency values at a major sports event relates to the 2002 World Snooker Championship in Sheffield (Shibli and Coleman 2005). During the nearly 100 hours of terrestrial coverage in the UK, the venue, 'The Crucible' (or 'Crucible Theatre'), was mentioned 493 times and 'Sheffield' was mentioned 123 times. The commercial cost of purchasing this exposure would have been £2,197,724 and £525,329 respectively, a total of over £2.7m. Despite its popularity as a measure of sponsorship effectiveness, media exposure does not necessarily equate to awareness. Indeed, Sleight (1989) observed that:

> While you can certainly get a guide to the visibility of your sponsorship and the potential for awareness among your target audience, you certainly cannot tell by measuring media mentions how many of your target audience saw and registered the mentions, nor how the viewers' attitude to you or your product has been influenced by the sponsorship.
>
> (Sleight 1989: 227)

The positive impact of sponsorship in creating awareness was perhaps most vividly demonstrated by the Cornhill Insurance Company's sponsorship of cricket. Before it committed itself to this sponsorship, research showed that unprompted spontaneous awareness of Cornhill Insurance among UK residents was less than 2 per cent, while after the five-year sponsorship it increased to 21 per cent. Cornhill's analysis of the annual benefits from its sponsorship in a typical year showed that during 140 hours of television coverage the company received 7,459 banner ratings on screen and 234 verbal mentions. In addition, there were 1,784 references on radio, 659 in the national press and 2,448 in the provincial press. The 250 tickets that Cornhill received for each Test Match were also a valuable aid in improving relations with brokers and customers. Cornhill estimated that its investment of £2 million (£1 million in event cost and £1 million backup cost) over the 5-year period, returned £10 million in increased annual premium income. It estimated that this would have cost £30 million in conventional advertising (Howard and Crompton 2004). However, the Cornhill case is likely to be atypical for two reasons. First, Cornhill did not engage in any form of communication except sponsorship and its associated advertising and, second, the company had a very low awareness level at the beginning of the sponsorship. These factors made it relatively easy to measure increases in awareness attributable to the sponsorship.

However, there are certain limitations when using brand recall as a measure of sponsorship effectiveness, as illustrated by a comparative study of the 1998 and 2006 FIFA World Cup tournaments (Nufer 2009). The study found that:

- Some official sponsors achieved only low recall values and improved their image only slightly – if at all.
- Some companies who were not engaged as official FWC sponsors were able to improve their recall and image values to the same extent as official sponsors.

Similar results emerged from telephone research by Performance Research Europe (2000) conducted in the two weeks following the 2000 European Football Championships. They reported that despite watching an average of 13 matches, many fans struggled to identify tournament sponsors, and were often confused by the presence of non-sponsors. During spontaneous sponsorship awareness questioning in the two weeks that followed the tournament's conclusion, 50 per cent of the fans in the sample were unable to name any sponsors involved. Only two out of 10 identified McDonald's and one out of 10 Coca-Cola and Pringles in an unprompted/top of the mind awareness approach. A prompted recall approach achieved a higher awareness with 85 per cent identifying Umbro, the England team kit sponsor whilst 75 per cent identified Carlsberg, another England, UK television coverage, and tournament sponsor. The research also showed that Carling, a non-sponsor, achieved nearly as much recall at 69 per cent and another non-sponsor, Nike, achieved 71 per cent which was ahead of tournament sponsor Adidas (70 per cent).

Ambush marketing is one possible explanation for these findings. More and more companies without any official status or communication rights regarding a specific event are trying to establish an association with the event using creative campaigns (Meenaghan 1994; Bortoluzzi and Frey 2002; Nufer 2005). Ambush marketers want to benefit from certain sporting events without being engaged as an official sponsor, thereby saving the sponsorship fee. Crompton (2004) notes that there has been a movement from evaluation measures of media exposure, awareness and image to intent to purchase, product trials and sales. Kodak corporation were one of the first major companies to shift their focus and the comments of one of their executives are probably representative of most major companies today:

> As a sponsor, I look to the promoter to come to us with ideas on how the property can, in our case, sell film. We are no longer satisfied with enhanced image, give us opportunities for onsite sales, well-developed hospitality packages, dealer tie-ins etc. and we'll listen.
>
> (Diggelman 1992: 5)

Perhaps the most desirable measure from a sponsor's perspective is the impact that a sponsorship investment has on sales. The following examples of Coca-Cola and Guinness serve to highlight how this can be measured:

> Coca-Cola uses sponsorship to gain prime retail display space. The axiom in the soft drink business is that if product goes on the floor, it sells. When Coke plans an event-themed promotion, it estimates the amount of incremental cases it will sell, factors in a profit ratio per case, and evaluates its return based on actual sales and the amount it spent on rights fees. For example, through its ties with NASCAR, Coke saw incremental sales of 30 million commemorative bottles and placement of 20,000 vending machines and point-of-purchase displays – bearing NASCAR themes – in retail outlets such as Home Depots and Wal-Marts.
>
> (IEG 1999)

> The Guinness company sponsored the 1999 Rugby World Cup. The company measured the impact of the sponsorship by comparing sales figures during the October/November time period when the event was held with sales in the same time period in the previous year. The percentage increases reported included: France 37 per cent, Australia 20 per cent, South Africa 24 per cent, Great Britain 17 per cent, Dubai 71 per cent and Malaysia 200 per cent.
>
> (Rines 2002)

Conclusions

This chapter has charted the explosive growth in sponsorship income to sport over the last 20 to 30 years. Though less in total than the amount raised through the sale of broadcasting rights, the rate of growth in sponsorship income has mirrored that from broadcasting. That is no coincidence. Sponsors are attracted to events that attract large television audiences. The summer Olympic Games and the Football World Cup attract the largest cumulative television audiences on the planet, with both events attracting the attention of over two-thirds of the world's population. As a result, these events are sponsored by global corporations aiming to enhance their global market position. The majority of these sponsors are non-sports corporations simply because most major global corporations are in the non-sports sector. These sponsors are not promoting sport. They are promoting their products that are marketed on a global basis with the events that have the largest global reach. There will continue to be a healthy market for sponsors at this top end of the events hierarchy. However, not all sports have events that achieve this level of global television coverage. For many sports, achieving major sponsorship deals can prove very difficult. Lower down the events hierarchy, sports are often faced with sponsors ending their sponsorship when faced with difficult economic conditions in their industrial environment. For these, sports sponsorship can be highly risky form of funding because of the volatility of sponsorship demand when sponsors are faced with the difficult trading conditions seen around the world since the global economic crisis of 2008–9.

8

GLOBALISATION OF THE SPORT MARKET: COSTS AND BENEFITS

Introduction

The previous chapters of this book have looked at how the sports business has changed since the 1980s to today and have pointed out the peculiar nature of this now global sports business. Such peculiarities include the following:

- Nike, the global leader of the sports-shoe market, sub-contracts nearly all of its production to Chinese and other Asian manufacturers yet still retains high profits and value added for the United States economy;
- A first-round snooker match in the 2009 World Championship had a live attendance of 893 people at the Crucible Theatre Sheffield (of which at least half were watching another match) and yet gained a live audience of over 110 million in China, a new record for a live TV audience for a snooker match. The match was Ding Junhui versus Liang Wenbo. The most famous match in snooker history, the 1985 World Championship final between Steve Davies and Dennis Taylor, attracted a live television audience of 18.5 million, mainly in the UK, which was then a new record. The average live UK TV audience for a World Championship match today is only around 2 million.
- Non-profit-making international governing bodies of sport, such as the IOC and FIFA, sell the broadcasting rights to their events for billions of dollars, most of which is profit.
- A domestic football competition, the English Premier League, is shown live in 211 countries and obtains over $2 billion from the sale of these international broadcasting rights.

The globalisation of the sport market has taken place over a relatively short time period since the early 1980s and is the culmination of a series of trends as identified by Westerbeek and Smith (2003):

- huge expansion in the number of broadcast hours devoted to sport on television and other media;
- increasing international standardisation of sports media output so the same sports pictures are broadcast across the world;
- increasing value of 'global sport properties', most notably athletes and major sports events;
- increasing market power of top global sports corporations, including sport-centred media companies;
- growth in the economic importance of sport both within national economies and globally;
- Increase in number of top global corporations, mainly from the non-sport sector, using sport as their major global sponsorship vehicle.

These are the trends we have seen in the earlier chapters of this book. In these chapters we have also seen the main beneficiaries of these trends: the major GSOs, the major athletes themselves, and the top global sports corporations. In this concluding chapter we look at the possible negative economic consequences of the globalisation of the sport market.

Negative economic consequences of the globalisation of sport

Thibault (2009) identified three major negative consequences from the globalisation of sport: the international division of labour with global sports corporations using labour from developing countries to manufacture sports clothing, shoes, and equipment; the migration of top athletes from their country of origin to countries willing to pay the highest salaries; and the increasing involvement of global media conglomerates in sport.

International division of labour

We have seen in the Nike case study in Chapter 5 that countries such as China have become the main producers of the global supply of sports equipment, clothing, and footwear. Nike's origins were in importing Japanese sports trainers into the American market. It then moved on to design and market its own brand. However, it has always contracted out the production of its products and still does, to factories outside the United States and predominantly in South East Asia. Other major brands such as Adidas and Puma have predominantly followed Nike's lead in this production model. Despite the attempts of these global sports corporations to devise codes of conduct and ethical guidelines for the factories in which their products are produced and hence to defend themselves against charges of labour exploitation, Thibault (2009) argues that such efforts 'have not, for the most part, translated into real positive changes in the operations of subcontractors and the treatment of workers in developing countries'. The reality is that a large number of the factories from which the global sport market sources its equipment, shoes and clothing still subjects its workers to 'low wages, long hours, lack of job security, and dismal and dangerous working conditions' (Thibault 2009: 5).

Migration of athletes

Several commentators (Bale and Maguire 1994; Bale and Sang 1996) have identified the problems with athletes migrating from their home countries to other countries offering higher financial rewards. The English Premier League attracts the best footballers from all over world. The football fans from the countries that these athletes leave are left with a lower average quality of player in their domestic football leagues and for some countries (e.g. Brazil) this can be a serious problem. However, at least these players represent their own country in major international tournaments such as the World Cup and then the experience of playing at a high level of competitive football abroad can prove a major bonus for the national team. So there is a trade-off between a reduction in quality of the domestic football against a possible increase in quality for the national team and therefore it is impossible to measure whether the net benefit is positive or negative.

There is no such trade-off when the athlete migrates to represent another country that is not his or her own country. This has happened repeatedly with top Kenyan distance runners. Bale and Maguire (1994) argued that the effect of such migration was to deskill the athletic pool of talent in Kenya. However, the potential welfare loss in the donor nation may be the major negative effect of such migration. We have seen in Chapter 3 that international sporting success is a public good. Governments spend substantial sums of money to generate success for their athletes. It takes a long time to produce a world-class athlete and governments throughout the world invest in such athletes as children, through their junior competitions, and finally at senior level. If that athlete then decides to represent another country, there is no rate of return on that investment in the home country. More importantly, sports fans in the country the athlete leaves are not able to enjoy to enjoy the public-good benefits of international success from the success of the leaving athlete. The very fact that another country has recruited the athlete is evidence that he or she is likely to generate such benefits, but in this case the benefit is transferred to the new country at the expense of the donor country.

Thibault (2009) points out that both with recruitment of athletes to domestic sports leagues and recruitment of athletes to represent countries, the direction of travel is from developing countries to developed, much richer, countries. The market power in these transactions is with the latter:

> From a global perspective, the acquisition of talent by developed nations' leagues and teams is largely carried out at the expense of developing nations' sports systems. The depletion of athletes with promising talent from developing countries is rarely replenished, in any form, by the organisations responsible for its depletion. Athletes are poached to enhance the quality of a sports team and league in affluent countries.
>
> (Thibault 2009: 8)

Global sport–media nexus

We have seen throughout the book how the globalisation of the sport market has created mutual dependencies between sport (both GSOs and the global sports corporations), broadcasters and sponsors and that the relationships between them have driven the globalisation process. Why then does Thibault (2009) argue that this global sport–media nexus is another negative economic consequence of the globalisation of sport? Thibault's main argument is twofold. The first relates to circumstances where sport has had to change to meet the demands of the media:

> for example, stoppage in play to allow commercial breaks in telecasts of events, changes in sport rules to enhance the appeal of the sport for fans, for sponsors, and for media … and the creation of new sports (and/or events) to target new audiences for TNCs and the media.
>
> (Thibault 2009: 10)

It is the takeover of sports teams by media conglomerates that Thibault sees as the main danger to sport, however, he names notable examples of media organisations ownership of sports properties including Disney (USA), News Corporation (Australia), Time Warner (USA), Vivendi SA (France), and Bertelsmann AG (Germany). Thibault points out the danger in such developments:

> As the number of media conglomerates increase their ownership of sport properties, we may see a decrease in the diversity in sport and sporting heritage. In addition, while media conglomerates increasingly gain control of sport properties, we can foresee a situation where only sports that can be commodified and commercialised will thrive. The value of sport will be determined by the size and composition of the audience available for media, advertisers, and sponsors.
>
> (Thibault 2009)

For these reasons, in some countries governments have intervened to prevent media conglomerates from taking over sports teams. One of the most notable examples of this was the intervention of the British government to prevent BSkyB taking over Manchester United in 1999. BSkyB was owned by News Corporation which had followed similar policies in both Australia and the USA. However, the Monopolies and Mergers Commission (MMC) found that there were serious threats to competition from the proposed takeover. At the time, BSkyB was the sole provider of live EPL content to the British market and Manchester United were the largest and most successful club in the EPL. The main reason the MMC recommended that the takeover should not go ahead is that it would give BSkyB an unfair advantage in the negotiation of the broadcasting rights to the EPL. In effect, it would give BSkyB a seat on both sides of the negotiating table, giving it an unfair advantage over other bidders for the rights. The government upheld the MMC recommendation and the takeover failed.

Conclusions

What we have seen throughout this book is that the globalisation of the sport market has taken certain sports organisations beyond the reach of regulation by national governments. The BSkyB takeover of Manchester United could still be prevented by the British government because it was covered by British competition legislation. European and Australian governments also intervene through their listed events legislation in the market for broadcasting rights owned by the GSOs such as the IOC and FIFA. This legislation prevents the GSOs from simply selling the rights to the highest bidder since events that are listed cannot be sold exclusively to pay-TV operators and must be shown on terrestrial channels covering most of the population. The GSOs do not like this because it restricts the market for the rights and hence restricts their income. The major pay-TV operators do not like it since it restricts their access to the top global events, most notably the Olympics and the World Cup in football, and potentially restricts their subscription base. Outside these two areas, however, national governments have little influence on the globalisation of the sport market. The whole point about the globalisation of sport is that it is supranational. GSOs, broadcasting companies and sponsors are operating in the world market for sport. The negative economic consequences of sports globalisation identified by Thibault (2009) are effectively market failures in the global sport market. Economics tells us that governments should intervene to correct such market failures. But there is no world government to carry out such interventions.

Perhaps, though, we should end on a much more positive note. Globalisation of the sport market has given us some very positive outcomes. Sports consumers worldwide get unprecedented coverage of all the major sports events taking place in the world. The sports fan, whether living in Australia, China, North America, or just about anywhere else with access to digital technology, can follow all the matches of top world teams such as Manchester United, Real Madrid or Barcelona. He or she can also follow every major golf tournament from both the American PGA tour and the European Tour. Similarly, other major sports events, wherever they take place, can be watched live by most of the world. Fans all over the world now have much greater knowledge of the top players in a wide range of sports and what is going on at the very top level in these sports. There are no national barriers to discussions about sport when fans from different countries meet. This broadening of knowledge may also have led to fewer security issues around major football events such as the World Cup and the European Championships with those so far in the twenty-first century being characterised by a carnival atmosphere with fans from different countries celebrating together at 'fanfest' sites set up in the host cities for fans without tickets.

Sport has also benefited from globalisation. Thirty years ago, most of the football clubs in the top division in England were virtually bankrupt. Most of their income came from gate receipts and gates had fallen consistently from reaching their peak in 1948. Football was a declining industry. Today, broadcasting revenue is the main source of income to the English Premier League closely followed by sponsorship and commercial income. The very fact that 211 countries receive live coverage of the EPL automatically increases their attractiveness to sponsors who seek such worldwide coverage. The same applies to the other major global sports events that have been discussed in this book. During the 2008–9 world recession sport was one of the few industries not to suffer a major cutback in revenue. Not only has sport received massive increases in income over recent years but this income has proved remarkably stable in challenging world economic conditions.

Sport has also massively increased its profile as an area of economic, social and cultural activity. It has to be taken seriously by those who do not even like sport and it is now a major global industry. In most developed economies it accounts for around 2 per cent of GDP, in some a lot more. A lot of the rise in the economic importance of sport in recent years is due to the developments we have discussed in this book.

Whatever the arguments relating to the costs and benefits of the globalisation of sport, there is no possibility of going back to the sort of national sport markets we had 30 years ago. It is unlikely that the pace of globalisation in the sport market will continue in the next 30 years at the rate it has over the last thirty due to the simple fact that it has already touched most of the world. It is certainly the case that new developments in technology and in sport will provide greater opportunities for further globalisation. Perhaps international agreements about governance of this global sport market may help correct for some of the global market imperfections we have identified here.

BIBLIOGRAPHY

Ahlert, G. and Preuss, H. (2010) 'Experiences in estimating the macroeconomic impact of mega tourism events: the case of hosting the Fifa Football World Cup Germany 2006', Johannes Gutenberg University of Mainz Institute of Sport Science Working Paper Series: Mainzer Papers on Sports Economics and Management, May.

Andreff, W. (1994) *The economic importance of sport in Europe: financing and economic impact,* Strasbourg: Council of Europe, Committee for the Development of Sport.

——(2008) 'Globalisation of the sports economy', *Diritto Ed Economia Dello Sport,* 4: 1–20.

Andreff, W. and Symanski, S. (2006), *Introduction: sport and economics,* in W. Andreff and S. Symanski (eds), *Handbook on the economics of sport,* Cheltenham: Edward Elgar.

Andrews, D.L. (2003) 'Sport and the transnationalizing media corporation', *Journal of Media Economics,* 16 (4): 235–51.

Baade, R. (1999) 'An analysis of why and how the United States Judiciary has interpreted the question of professional sports and economic development', in C. Jeanrenaud (ed.), *The economic impact of sports events,* Neuchatel: CIES.

Bale, J. and Maguire, J. (1994) *The global sports arena: Athletic talent migration in an interdependent world,* London: Frank Cass.

Bale, J. and Sang, J. (1996) *Kenyan running: Movement culture, geography and global change,* London: Frank Cass.

Barnett, S. (1990) *Games and sets: the changing face of sport on television,* London: British Film Institute.

Barney, R.K., Wenn, S.R. and Martyn, S.G. (2002) *Selling the five rings: the International Olympic Committee and the rise of Olympic commercialism,* Salt Lake City: University of Utah Press.

Beijing Review (2008) 'Facilities: completion of Olympic stadiums and venues', Online, Available http://www.bjreview.com.cn/olympic/txt/2008-08/01/content_137599.htm

Bensch, B. (2007) 'Real Madrid has top soccer brand value', Online, Available http://www.bloomberg.com/apps/news?pid=newsarchive&sid=a6OsxihKITtE&refer=latin_america (accessed 10 January 2010).

Berkshire Encyclopaedia of World Sport (2005) *Commodification and commercialization,* Vol. 1, Great Barrington, MA: Berkshire Publishing Group.

Bevan, C. and Stevenson, J. (2008) 'Premier League going global', Online, Available http://news.bbc.co.uk/sport1/hi/football/eng_prem/7232378.stm (accessed 27 February 2010).

Bianchini, F. and Schwengel, H. (1991) 'Re-imagining the city', in J. Comer and S. Harvey (eds), *Enterprise and heritage: Crosscurrents of national culture,* London: Routledge.

Bird, P. (1982) 'The demand for league football', *Applied Economics*, 14: 637–49.

BOCOG (2006) 'General policy for volunteers for the Beijing Olympic and Paralympic Games', 27 August, Online, Available http://en.beijing2008.cn/26/82/article212038226.shtml

——(2007) 'In Beijing, Olympics prompt infrastructure development and better quality of life', 25 November, Online, Available http://en.beijing2008.cn/news/dynamics/headlines/n214204287.shtml

——(2008) Press conference: Beijing Olympics cultural activities, 28 July, Online, Available http://en.beijing2008.cn/news/n214083931.shtml

——(2008) 'Press conference on cost-efficiency Olympic Games URL', 1 August, Online, Available http://en.beijing2008.cn/live/pressconference/mpc/n214495413.shtml

Boone, L.E. and Kurtz, D.L. (2010) *Contemporary business*, Oxford: Wiley-Blackwell.

Bortoluzzi, E. and Frey, H. (2002) *Sponsoring. Der Leitfaden für die Praxis*, 3rd edn, Bern: Haupt.

Bramwell, B. (1991) 'Sheffield: tourism planning in an industrial city', *Insights*, March: 23–8.

——(1995) 'Event tourism in Sheffield: A sustainable approach to urban development?', unpublished paper, Centre for Tourism, Sheffield Hallam University.

Brookes, B. and Madden, P. (1995) *The globe-trotting sports shoe*, London: Christian Aid.

Brown, J. (2008) 'Carrying the torch', *Civil Engineering Magazine*, August.

Buchanan, J.M. (1965) 'An economic theory of clubs', *Economica*, 32 (125): 1–14.

Burns, J.P.A., Hatch, J.H. and Mules, F.J. (1986) *The Adelaide Grand Prix: The impact of a special event*, Adelaide: The Centre for South Australian Economic Studies.

Chalip, L. (2004) 'Beyond impact: A general model for host community event leverage', in B.W. Ritchie and D. Adair (eds), *Sport tourism: Interrelationships, impacts and issues*, Clevedon, UK: Channel View Publications.

Chalip, L. and Costa, C. (2005) 'Sport event tourism and the destination brand: towards a general theory', *Sport in Society*, 8 (2): 218–37.

Chalip, L., Green, B.C. and Hill, B. (2003) 'Effects of sport event media on destination image and intention to visit', *Journal of Sport Management*, 17: 214–34.

China Daily (2008) 'Beijing Olympics attracts record 4.7 billion TV viewers', 6 September.

——(2009) 'Bird's Nest takes gold in tourism stakes', 1 October.

Chinanet (2008) 'Beijing Olympics will not affect momentum of China's economy', Online, Available http: china.com.cn, 2008-08-22.

China Youth Daily (2008) '97.8% people support public opening of Birds Nest and Water Cube with discount'.

Clarke, R. (2002) *The future of sports broadcasting rights*, Sport Business Group Limited.

Clifford, M. (1992) 'Nike roars', *Far Eastern Economic Review*, 55 (44): 58–9.

Coalter, F., Long, J. and Duffield, B. (1986) *Rationale for public sector investment in leisure*, London: Sports Council.

Cone, J. (2006) 'Soccer World Cup final had sport's largest TV audience of 2006', Online, Available http://bloomberg.com/apps/news?pid=20601077&sid=aOYdMOmxoV4c&refer=intsports retrieved (accessed 2 January 2011).

Craig, S. (2002) *Sports and games of the ancients*, Westport, CT: Greenwood Press.

Crompton, J.L. (1995) 'Factors that have stimulated the growth of sponsorship of major events', *Festival Management and Event Tourism*, 3: 97–101.

——(2001) 'Public subsidies to professional team sport facilities in the USA', in C. Gratton and I. Henry (eds), *Sport in the city: The role of sport in economic and social regeneration*, London: Routledge.

——(2004) 'Conceptualization and alternate operationalizations of the measurement of sponsorship effectiveness in sport', *Leisure Studies*, 23 (3): 267–81.

Czinkota, M.R. and Ronkainen, I.A. (2007) *International marketing*, 8th edn, Mason, OH: Thomson South-Western.

Davies, T.R. (2008) 'The rise and fall of transnational civil society: The evolution of international non-governmental organizations since 1839', Online, Available http://www.city.ac.uk/intpol/

dps/WorkingPapers/T_Davies%20The%20Rise%20and%20Fall%20of%20Transnational%20Civil%20Society.pdf (accessed 8 January 2010).

DCMS (2009) *Review of free-to-air listed events: Report by the independent advisory panel to the Secretary of State for culture, media and sport*, London: Department of Culture, Media, and Sport (DCMS).

Deloitte (2005) *Annual review of football finance*, Manchester: Deloitte and Touche.

——(2006) *Annual review of football finance*, Manchester: Deloitte and Touche.

Diggelman, R. (1992) 'The bottom line on sponsorship', *Sponsorship Report*, 11 (24): 4–5.

Dobson, N., Gratton, C. and Holliday, S. (1997) *Football came home: The economic impact of Euro 96*, Sheffield: Leisure Industries Research Centre.

Dong, J. and Mangan, J. (2008) 'Beijing Olympics legacies: Certain intentions and certain and uncertain outcomes', *The International Journal of the History of Sport*, 25 (14): 2019–40.

Dunning, E., Malcolm, D. and Waddington, I. (2006) *Sport histories: Figurational studies in the development of modern sport*, London: Routledge.

Dunning, J.H. (1988) *Explaining international production*, London: Unwin Hyman.

Economist, The (2011) 'The awfulness of FIFA: An embarrassment to the beautiful game', Online, Available http://www.economist.com/node/18774796 (accessed 2 June 2011).

Elias, N. and Dunning, E. (1986) *Quest for excitement: Sport and leisure in the civilising process*, Oxford: Blackwell.

EPL (2010) 'Research and Insight 2010/11', Online, Available http://fansurvey.premierleague.com/ (accessed 18 April 2011).

——(2011) 'History of the Premier League', Online, Avaliable http://www.premierleague.com/page/History/0,12306,00.html (accessed 24 November 2011).

ESPN (2010a) 'ESPN in Asia and Japan', Online, Available: http://espnmediazone3.com/wpmu/europe/ (accessed 1 December 2011).

ESPN (2010b) 'ESPN in Europe', Online, Available: http://espnmediazone3.com/wpmu/asia_japan/ (accessed 1 December 2011).

ESPN (2011) 'ESPN International fact sheet', Online, Available: http://espnmediazone3.com/wpmu/europe/espn-international-fact-sheet/ (accessed 1 December 2011).

FGG (2009) 'We are athletes, coaches, sports and cultural leaders, and community supporters', Online, Available http://www.gaygames.net/index.php?id=4 (accessed 25 September 2009).

FIFA (2007) 'The FIFA sponsorship programme 2007–14', Online, Available http://www.fifa.com/worldcup/archive/southafrica2010/organisation/marketing/ (accessed 24 January 2011).

Forster, J. and Pope, N.K.L. (2004) *The political economy of global sporting organisations*, London: Routledge.

Fraser, A. (2009) 'US$29.182 billion spent on sport in first quarter of 2009', Online, Available http://www.sportspromedia.com/deals/_a/sport_fights_recession_us29.182_billion_and_counting/ (accessed 24 November 2009).

Garcia, S. (1993) 'Barcelona und die Olympischen Spiele', in H. Häussermann and W. Siebel (eds), Festivalisierung der Stadtpolitik. Stadtentwicklung durch große Projekte, in Leviathan. Zeitschrift für Sozialwissenschaft, Opladen.

Getz, D. (1991) *Festivals, special events, and tourism*, New York: Van Nostrand Reinhold.

Girginov, V. and Hills, L. (2008) 'A sustainable sports legacy: creating a link between the London Olympics and sports participation', *International Journal of the History of Sport*, 25 (14): 2091–116.

Gitman, L. and McDaniel, C. (2009) *The essentials of the future of business*, Andover: Cengage Learning.

Gratton, C. (2004) 'Sport, health and economic benefit', in N. Rowe (ed.), *Driving up participation: The challenge for sport*, London: Sport England.

Gratton, C. and Taylor, P. (1985) *Sport and recreation: an economic analysis*, London: E and FN Spon.

——(1987) *Leisure industries – an overview*, London: Comedia.

——(1991) *Government and the economics of sport*, Harlow: Longman.

——(2000) *Economics of sport and recreation*, Abingdon: Routledge.

Gratton, C. and Solberg, H. (2007) *The economics of sports broadcasting*, Abingdon: Routledge.

Gratton, C. and Preuss, H. (2008) 'Maximising Olympic impacts by building up legacies', *The International Journal of the History of Sport*, 25 (14): 1922–38.

Gratton, C., Shibli, S. and Dobson, N. (2000) 'The economic importance of major sports events', *Managing Leisure*, 5 (1): 17–28.

——(2001) 'The role of major sports events in the economic regeneration of cities', in C. Gratton and I. Henry (eds), *Sport in the city: The role of sport in economic and social regeneration*, London: Routledge.

Guo Tingting (2001) 'How was the support of 94.9% for Beijing Olympic bidding calculated?', Huaxi Urban Post, 20 February.

Hall, C.M. (1992) *Hallmark tourist events: Impacts, management and planning*, London: Belhaven Press.

——(2004) 'Sports tourism and urban regeneration', in B.W. Ritchie and D. Adair (eds), *Sports tourism: Interrelationships, impacts and issues*, Clevedon: Channelview Publications.

——(2006) 'Urban entrepreneurship, corporate interests and sports mega-events: the thin policies of competitiveness within the hard outcomes of neoliberalism', in J. Horne and W. Manzenreiter (eds), *Sports mega-events: Social scientific analyses of a global phenomenon*, Oxford: Blackwell.

Hawtin, L. (2004) 'Imperial Leather sponsorship wins the 2002 Commonwealth Games', in G. Masterman, *Sponsorship: For a return on investment*, Oxford: Elsevier/Butterworth–Heinemann.

Held, D. and McGrew, A.G. (2002) *Governing globalization: Power, authority and global governance*, Cambridge: Polity Press.

Holmes, S. (2004) 'The new Nike', *Business Week*, 20 September.

Holt, R. (1989) *Sport and the British: A modern history*, Oxford: Clarendon Press.

Horn, M. and Buken, K. (1999) 'Measuring the impact of sponsorship', *International Journal of Sports Marketing and Sponsorship*, September/October.

Horne, J. and Manzenreiter, W. (2006) *Sports mega-events: Social scientific analyses of a global phenomenon*, Oxford: Blackwell.

——(2007) *Football goes east: Business, culture and the people's game in East Asia*, London: Routledge.

Howard, D.R. and Crompton, J.L. (2004) *Financing sport*, 2nd edn, Morgantown, WV: Fitness Information Technology.

IAAF (2010) 'Official IAAF partners', Online, Available http://www.iaaf.org/aboutiaaf/partners/index.html (accessed 9 February 2010).

IOC (2007) 'Olympic charter', Online, Available http://www.olympic.org/Documents/olympic_charter_en.pdf (accessed 24 November 2009).

——(2008) 'Olympic marketing fact file', Online, Available http://www.olympic.org/Documents/marketing_fact_file_en.pdf (accessed 15 January 2011).

——(2010) 'The Olympic movement', Online, Available http://www.olympic.org/Documents/Reference_documents_Factsheets/The_Olympic_Movement.pdf (accessed 15 February 2010).

IEG (1999) 'Evaluation leads Coke to new sponsorship strategy', *Sponsorship Report*, 18 (13): 4–5.

——(2002) 'IEG/Performance research survey reveals what matters to sponsors', *Sponsorship Report*, 21 (7): 4–5.

IEG (2009) 'Sponsorship spending recedes for first time; better days seen ahead', *Sponsorship Report*, 28 (24): 1–5.

Jennett, N. (1984) 'Attendances, uncertainty of outcome and policy in the Scottish Football League', *Scottish Journal of Political Economy*, 31 (2): 176–98.

Jinxia, D. and Mangan, J.A. (2008) 'Beijing Olympic legacies: Certain intentions and certain and uncertain outcomes', *The International Journal of the History of Sport*, 25 (14): 2019–40.

Jinghua Shibao (2008) 'Over 1500 post-games BOCOG workers attending job fair with 1753 jobs offered', 19 October.

Jones, H. (1989) *The Economic impact and importance of sport: a European study*, Strasbourg: Council of Europe.

Kasimati, E. (2003) 'Economic aspects and the Summer Olympics: a review of related research', *International Journal of Tourism Research*, 5: 433–44.

Keohane, R. and Nye, J. (2000) 'Introduction', in J.S. Nye and J.D. Donahue (eds), *Governance in a Globalizing World*, Washington: Brookings Institution Press. Online, Available http://www.ccebook.net/author/

Kexel, P. (2010) 'Galactic revenues – How Real Madrid captured the money champions league', Online, Available http://idw-online.de/pages/en/news373489 (accessed 15 November 2011).

Klein, N. (2000) *No logo*, London: Flamingo.

Law, A., Harvey, J. and Kemp, S. (2002) 'The global sport mass media oligopoly: the three usual suspects and more', *International Review for the Sociology of Sport*, 37 (3–4): 279–302.

Lee, J. (2005) 'Marketing and promotion at the Olympics', *The Sport Journal*, Online, Available http://www.thesportjournal.org/article/marketing-and-promotion-olympic-games (accessed 8 December 2011).

Lewis, R.D. (2006) *When cultures collide. Leading across cultures*, Boston, MA London: Nicholas Brealey.

Li, H. (2008) 'China features: Olympics boosts Chinese language promotion', Online, Available http://www.chinaconsulate.org.nz/eng/xwdt/t513660.htm

Lipsman, A. (2007) 'Top European football clubs have global fan base', Online, Available http://www.comscore.com/Press_Events/Press_Releases/2007/05/European_Football_Clubs (accessed 15 November 2011).

Liu, D. (2004) 'Globalisation of ideas', PhD Dissertation, Shanghai International Studies University.

Liu, D. and Gratton, C. (2010) 'The impact of mega-sporting events on live spectators' Images of a host city: A case-study of the Shanghai F1 Grand Prix', *Tourism Economics*, 16 (3): 629–46.

MacAloon, J.J. (2011) 'Scandal and governance: inside and outside the IOC Commission', *Sport in Society*, 14 (3): 292–308.

McComb, D.G. (2004) *Sports in world history*, London: Routledge.

Maguire, J., Jarvie, G., Mansfield, L. and Bradley, J. (2002) *Sport worlds: A sociological perspective*, Leeds: Human Kinetics.

Maidment, P. (2006) 'For the sponsors, huge global exposure', in B. Smart, *The sport star: modern sport and the cultural economy of sporting celebrity*, London: Sage

Malcolmson, R.W. (1973) 'Popular recreations in English society', 1700–1850, Cambridge: Cambridge University Press.

Mandell, R.D. (1984) *Sport: a cultural history*, New York: Columbia University Press.

Mangan, J. (2008) 'Prologue: guarantees of global goodwill: post-Olympic legacies – too many limping white elephants?' *The International Journal of the History of Sport*, 25 (14): 1869–83.

Martzke, R. (2003) 'NBC keeps rights for Olympic broadcasts through 2012', Online, Available http://www.usatoday.com/sports/olympics/2003-06-06-nbc_x.htm (accessed 15 February 2010).

Mason, T. (1980) *Association football and English society, 1863–1915*, Brighton: Harvester Press.

Masterman, G. (2004) *Strategic sports event management: An international approach*, Oxford: Butterworth-Heinemann.

——(2007) *Sponsorship: For a return on investment*. Oxford: Elsevier/Butterworth-Heinemann.

——(2009) *Strategic sports event management: an Olympic edition*, Oxford: Butterworth-Heinemann.

Masterman, G. and Wood, E.H. (2006) *Innovative marketing communications: Strategies for the events industry*. Oxford: Elsevier/Butterworth–Heinemann.

Meenaghan, J. A. (1991) 'The role of sponsorship in the marketing communications mix', *International Journal of Advertising*, 10: 35–7

Meenaghan, T. (1994) 'Point of view: Ambush marketing: Immoral or Imaginative practice?', *Journal of Advertising Research*, 34 (9/10): 77–88.

Monopolies and Mergers Commission (MMC) (1999) *British Sky Broadcasting PLC and Manchester United PLC: a report on the proposed merger*, London: The Stationery Office.

Mules, T. and Faulkner, B. (1996) 'An economic perspective on major events', *Tourism Economics*, 12 (2): 107–17.

Müller, N. (2006) 'The idea of peace as Coubertin's vision for the Modern Olympic Movement: development and pedagogic consequences', *The Sport Journal*, 9 (1).

——(2009) 'The idea of peace as Coubertin's vision for the modern Olympic movement: Development and pedagogic consequences', *The Sport Journal*, Online, Available http://www.thesportjournal.org/article/idea-peace-coubertins-vision-modern-olympic-movement-development-and-pedagogic-consequences (accessed 24 November 2009).

NAO Report (2009) Follow-up audit findings on the revenues and expenditures of the Beijing Olympics and the construction of Olympic venues, report of National Audit Office of China, no. 8 of 2009 (Serial No. 40).

Neale, W.C. (1964) 'The peculiar economics of professional sports', *Quarterly Journal of Economics*, 78 (1): 1–14.

Nufer, G. (2005) 'Ambush marketing – Angriff aus dem Hinterhalt oder eine Alternative zum Sportsponsoring?', in H.D. Horch, G. Hovemann, S. Kaiser and K. Viebahn (eds), *Perspektiven des Sportmarketing. Besonderheiten, Herausforderungen, Tendenzen*, Cologne: Institut für Sportökonomie und Sportmanagement, 209–27.

——(2009) 'How effective is the sponsorship of global sports events? A comparison of the FIFA World Cups in 2006 and 1998', *International Journal of Sports Marketing and Sponsorship*, July: 303–19.

Olympics.org. (2009) 'Official website of the Olympic Movement', Online, Available http://www.olympic.org/ (accessed 15 November 2011).

Ornstein, D. and Soneji, P. (2008) 'Pros and cons of global premier plan', Online, Available http://news.bbc.co.uk/sport1/hi/football/eng_prem/7233395.stm (accessed 20 February 2011).

Penrose, E.T. (1959) *The theory of the growth of the firm*, Oxford: Basil Blackwell.

People's Daily (2008) 'BOCOG Official Liu Jian: 1.7 million volunteers welcoming Olympics with smile People's Daily', August. BOCOG Official Liu Jian: 1.7 million volunteers welcoming Olympics with smile

People's Daily Online (2001) 'Olympic bidding success spurs English language fever in China', 29 July, Online, Available http://english.peopledaily.com.cn/200107/29/eng20010729_76042.html

——(2008) 'Chinese Culture Reading holds premiere release, 19 June, Online, Available http://english.people.com.cn/90001/90782/90873/6433217.html

——(2009) 'Post-Olympic road of Bird's Nest', Online, Available http://english.peopledaily.com.cn/90001/90782/90873/6690945.html

Performance Research Europe (2000) 'British football fans can't recall Euro 2000 sponsors', Online, Available http://www.performanceresearch.com/euro-2000-sponsorship.htm (accessed 15 January 2011).

Phillips, R. (1999) 'Big business demands a corporate Olympics', Online, Available http://www.wsws.org/articles/1999/mar1999/olym-m16.shtml (accessed 9 February 2010).

Plowright, M. (2008) 'The agony and the ecstasy', Online, Available http://www.cibmagazine.com.cn/Print/Show.asp?id=535&the_agony_and_the_ecstasy.html (accessed 17 February 2011).

Preuss, H. (2004) *The economics of staging the Olympics. A comparison of the games 1972–2008*, Cheltenham: Edward Elgar.

Preuss, H. and Messing, M. (2002) 'Auslandstouristen bei den Olympischen Spielen in Sydney 2000', in A. Dreyer (ed.), *Tourismus im Sport*, Wiesbaden: Deutscher Universitäts-Verlag.

Reference for Business (2011) ' Real Madrid C.F.', Online, Available http://www.referenceforbusiness.com/history/Qu-Ro/Real-Madrid-C-F.html (accessed 16 November 2011).

Reid, D.A. (1967) 'The decline of Saint Monday, 1966–1876', *Past and Present*, 71 (May).

Rines, S. (2002) 'Guinness Rugby World Cup sponsorship: a global platform for meeting business objectives', *International Journal of Sports Marketing and Sponsorship,* December/January: 449–64.

Ritchie, J.R.B. (1984) 'Assessing the impact of hallmark event: conceptual and research issues', *Journal of Travel Research,* 23 (1): 2–11.

Ritchie, J.R.B. and Aitken C.E. (1984) 'Assessing the impacts of the 1988 Olympic Winter Games: the research program and initial results', *Journal of Travel Research,* 22 (3): 17–25.

——(1985) 'OLYMPULSE II – evolving resident attitudes towards the 1988 Olympics', *Journal of Travel Research,* 23 (Winter): 28–33.

——(1987) 'OLYMPULSE III/IV: a mid term report on resident attitudes concerning the 1988 Olympic Winter Games', *Journal of Travel Research,* 26 (Summer): 18–26.

——(1990) 'OLYMPULSE VI: a post-event assessment of resident reaction to the XV Olympic Winter Games', *Journal of Travel Research,* 28 (3): 14–23.

Ritchie, J.R.B. and Smith, B.H. (1991) 'The impact of a mega event on host region awareness: a longitudinal study', *Journal of Travel Research,* 30 (1): 3–10.

Roche, M. (1992) 'Mega-event planning and citizenship: Problems of rationality and democracy in Sheffield's Universiade 1991', *Vrijetijd en Samenleving,* 10 (4): 47–67.

——(1994) 'Mega-events and urban policy', *Annals of Tourism Research,* 21 (1): 1–19.

——(2006) 'Mega-events and modernity revisited: globalisation and the case of the Olympics', in J. Horne and W. Manzenreiter (eds), *Sports mega-events: social scientific analyses of a global phenomenon,* Oxford: Wiley-Blackwell.

Rosenau, J.N. (1992) 'Normative challenges in a turbulent world', *Ethics and International Affairs,* 6 (1) 1–19.

Sanahuja, R. (2002) 'Olympic city – the city strategy 10 years after the Olympic Games in 1992', paper delivered to the International Conference on Sports Events and Economic Impact, Copenhagen.

Scambler, G. (2005) *Sport and society: History, power and culture,* Maidenhead: Open University Press.

Schimmel, K.S. (2001) 'Sport matters: urban regime theory and urban regeneration in the late capitalist era', in C. Gratton and I. Henry (eds), *Sport in the city: The role of sport in economic and social regeneration,* London and New York: Routledge.

Schwartz, E. and Hunter, J. (2008) *Advanced theory and practice in Sport marketing,* Oxford: Elsevier/Butterworth-Heinemann.

Scitovsky, T. (1976) *The joyless economy,* Oxford: Oxford University Press.

Segal-Horn, S. (1989) 'The globalisation of service firms', in P. Jones (ed.), *Management in service firms,* Harlow: Prentice Hall.

Shibli, S. (2001) 'Using an understanding of the behaviour patterns of key participant groups to predict the economic impact of major sports events', *Proceedings for the Ninth EASM Congress,* Vitoria-Gasteiz, Spain.

——(2008) 'The elite sport legacy of the 2008 Olympic and Paralympic Games', *Proceedings of the Sixteenth EASM Conference 2008,* Bayreuth/Heidelberg.

Shibli, S. and Coleman, R. (2005) 'Economic impact and place marketing evaluation: A case study of the world snooker championship', *International Journal of Event Management Research,* 1 (1): 13–29.

Shibli, S. and Bingham, J. (2008) 'A forecast of the performance of China in the Beijing Olympic Games and the underlying performance management issues', *Managing Leisure,* 13 (3–4): 272–92.

Sleight, S. (1989) *Sponsorship: What is it and how to use it,* Maidenhead: McGraw Hill.

Sloane, P. (1971) 'The economics of professional football: the football club as a utility maximiser', *Scottish Journal of Political Economy,* 18: 121–46.

Smart, B. (2005) *The sport star: Modern sport and the cultural economy of sporting celebrity,* London: Sage.

——(2007) 'Not playing around: Global capitalism, modern sport and consumer culture', *Global Networks,* 7 (2): 113–34.

Smit, B. (2006) *Pitch invasion: Adidas and the making of modern sport*, London: Allen Lane.

Smith, A. (2001) 'Sporting a new image?', in C. Gratton and I. Henry (eds), *Sport in the city: The role of sport in economic and social regeneration*, London and New York: Routledge.

——(2002) 'Reimaging the city: The impact of sport initiatives on tourists' images of urban destinations', PhD dissertation, Sheffield Hallam University.

——(2005) 'Re-imaging the city: The value of sport initiatives', *Annals of Tourism Research*, 32 (1): 217–36.

Snyder, C.R., Lassegard, M.A. and Ford, C.E. (1986) 'Distancing after group success and failure: Basking in reflected glory and cutting off reflected failure', *Journal of Personality and Social Psychology*, 51 (2): 382–8.

Solberg, H.A. and Preuss, H. (2007) 'Major sporting events and long-term tourism impacts', *Journal of Sport Management*, 21 (2): 213–34.

Sport Business (2006) 'World Cup viewing figures soar', Online, Available http://www.sportbusiness.com/news/159988/world-cup-viewing-figures-soar (accessed 13 February 2010).

——(2008) 'ESPN's brand of gold', Online, Available http://www.sportbusiness.com/print-edition/espns-brand-gold (accessed 8 December 2011).

——(2010a) 'Global TV sports rights', Online, Available http://www.sportbusiness.com/downloads/global-tv-sports-rights-171459 (accessed 15 January 2011).

——(2010b) 'The sports sponsorship market', Online, Available http://www.sportbusiness.com/downloads/the-sports-sponsorship-market-171464 (accessed 15 January 2011).

Sports Council (1983) *Swimming in the community*, London: Sports Council.

Stokvis, R. (2000) 'Globalization, commercialization and individualization: Conflicts and changes in elite athletics', *Culture, Sport, Society* 3 (1): 22–34.

Sugden, J. and Tomlinson, A. (1998) *FIFA and the contest for world football*, Cambridge: Polity Press.

Sun, D. (2007) Zhongguo shenao qinli ji [Experiencing China's Olympic bid], Dangdai [Contemporary], 4.

Talking Retail (2010) 'Rubicon sponsors a summer of cricket on Sky Sports', Online, Available http://www.talkingretail.com/products/product-news/rubicon-sponsors-a-summer-of-cricket-on-sky-sports (accessed 15 February 2011).

Thibault, L. (2009) 'Gobalization of sport: An inconvenient truth', *Journal of Sport Management*, 23: 1–20.

Thompson, E.P. (1967) 'Time, work discipline and industrial capitalism', *Past and Present*, 38 (December).

Todreas, T.M. (1999) 'Value creation and branding in television's digital age', Westport, CT: Quorum Books.

Tomlinson, A. (2005) 'Olympic survivals: The Olympic Games as a global phenomenon', in L. Allison, *The global politics of sport: The role of global institutions in sport*, London: Routledge.

Toohey, K. and Veal, A.J. (2007) *The Olympic Games: a social science perspective*, Oxon: CAB International.

UK Sport (2004) 'Measuring success 2', Online, Available http://www.uksport.gov.uk/docLib/Publications/Measuring-Success-2.pdf (accessed 24 April 2011).

Viscusi, G. (2006) 'Visa, MasterCard feud drives World Cup rights to $1.1 Billion', Online, Available http://www.bloomberg.com/apps/news?pid=newsarchive&sid=aMFQ55yLXSEY (accessed 10 January 2011).

Wallace, I. (1990) *The global economic system*, London: Unwin Hyman.

Walmsley, D.J. and Young, M. (1998) 'Effects of hosting sport event on destination brand: a test of co-branding and match-up models', *Journal of Travel Research*, 36 (3) 65–9.

Walsh, A. and Giulianotti, R. (2002) 'This sporting mammon! A moral critique of the commodification of sport', *Journal of the Philosophy of Sport* XXVIII (1), 53–77.

WADA (2009), 'About WADA', Online, Available: http://www.wada-ama.org/en/About-WADA/ (accessed 18 November 2009).

Weisbrod, B.A. (1978) *The voluntary non-profit sector*, Lexington, MA: Lexington Books.

——(1988) *The non-profit economy*, Cambridge, MA: Harvard University Press.

——(1998) *To profit or not to profit: the commercial transformation of the nonprofit sector*, Cambridge: Cambridge University Press.

Westerbeek, H. and Smith, A. (2003) *Sport business in the global marketplace*, Basingstoke: Palgrave Macmillan.

Whannel, G. (2005) 'The five rings and the small screen: television, sponsorship, and new media in the Olympic Movement', in K. Young and K.B. Wamsley (eds), *Global Olympics: historical and sociological studies of the modern Games*, London: Elsevier.

Wild, L. (2006) 'Strengthening global civil society', Online, Available http://docs.google.com/viewer?a=v&q=cache:uEIcnmULZYwJ:www.ngo.ee/orb.aw/class%3Dfile/action%3Dpreview/id%3D9230/Strengthening%2Bglobal%2Bcivil%2Bsociety.pdf+global+civil+society+ingo&hl=en&sig=AHIEtbQCf2PPz_v7fHxdUZwaVbA9G1p0Wg (accessed 8 January 2010).

Williams, O. (2009) 'Where the Premier League's players come from', Online, Available http://news.bbc.co.uk/sport/hi/football/eng_prem/8182090.stm#list (accessed 26 January 2011).

Willigan, G. (1992) 'High performance marketing: nike', *Harvard Business Review*, 70 (4): 90–101.

Wilson, J. (2007) 'Premier League is world's favourite league', Online, Available http://www.telegraph.co.uk/sport/football/2325057/Premier-League-is-worlds-favourite-league.html (accessed 13 February 2010).

Wolsey, C. and Abrams, J. (2001) *Understanding the leisure and sport industry*, London: Longman.

Xing, X. and Chalip, L. (2006) 'Effects of hosting a sport event on destination brand: A test of co-branding and match-up models', *Sport Management Review*, 9: 49–78.

Xinhuanet (2008) 'Facts and figures released by IOC', 26 November.

Xinjing Daily (2008) '1.7 million volunteers for Beijing Olympics well Prepared', 2 August.

Xu, X. (2006) 'Modernizing China in the Olympic spotlight: China's national identity and the 2008 Beijing Olympiad', *Sociological Review*, 54: 90–107.

Xu, G. (2008) *Olympic dreams: China and sports 1895–2008*, Cambridge, MA: Harvard University Press.

INDEX

Note: page number in *italic* type refer to Figures; those in **bold** type refer to Tables. Individual Olympic Games are entered under the name of the city (e.g. Beijing, London), not under 'Olympic Games'.